HEART BREAKS

A CARDIOLOGIST REVEALS THE SECRET LANGUAGE OF HEALING

Dr Mimi Guarneri

Introduction by
Dr Naresh Trehan

Let Knowledge Spread

Vitasta Publishing Pvt. Ltd.
2/15, Ansari Road, Daryaganj,

info@vitastapublishing.com

ISBN 81-89766-32-5
ISBN 978-93-80828-40-4

Cover & Layout Design by Vitasta Publishing Pvt. Ltd.
Printed by Vits Press.

Times Group Books
(A division of Bennett, Coleman and Company Limited)
Times Annexe, Express Building
9-10 Bahadur Shah Zafar Marg.

To

My patients, who taught me that the heart is more than a pump.
My family, who taught me all things are possible.
And Rauni Prittinen King, who taught me the difference
between being a physician and being a healer.

Contents

Contents

Introduction

By Dr. Naresh Trehan

Heart is not just a biological organ. It interacts with the environment like no other human organ. While medicine is useful for keeping the ailing hearts alive and kicking, more than half the battle can be won by altering the socio-economic and cultural settings in which the heart operates. People have successfully tried to keep their hearts healthy by changing their lifestyles and by following stress management techniques.

While a human body can survive without brain, it cannot survive without a heart. It is formed in the most initial stages of development and stops functioning only when all other organs have failed to deliver, with the exception of a heart failure, where in other organs fail because of the failure of the heart. When a woman conceives a baby, one of the most initial things that give her the feeling of being home to a developing human is the foetus's heartbeat. Therefore, it becomes all the more important to protect that organ of the body which experiences all the stages of human life more than any other organ.

While there is a raised consciousness about heart problems in the West, it is very poor in India even though the country is more vulnerable to cardiovascular diseases (CVD) than other countries. The World Health Organization (WHO) has estimated that by 2010, about 60 per cent of the world's cardiac patients would be Indians. Why is this so?

Why India, even when it is fast climbing the ladder of economic growth and prosperity? Even though HIV has become a new scourge in India, the number of people falling prey to CVD is alarming.

More troubling is the startling revelation that nearly 50 per cent of the CVD-related deaths in India occur below the age of 70. In the West it is merely 22 per cent. This proves wrong the assumption that CVD is age specific. A study has warned that unless we change our lifestyle, more than half of the world's cardiac patients by the middle of the 21st century would be from India.

The unusual susceptibility of South Asians in general and Indians in particular to the CVD can easily be traced to lifestyle issues such as diet, rapid urbanization and genes. The common denominator is an increasingly sedentary lifestyle. Earlier, irrespective of what we ate, the high demands on our life kept the body moving. The situation has changed with a decrease in physical activity and an increase in food intake. One would not disagree that given a choice we Indians would drive to the bathroom. Increased dependence on various modern gadgets has allowed us to be more indulgent with ourselves. But it has robbed us of the little opportunities we used to get to exercise our lax bones. A regular exercise schedule can help people keep heart diseases at an arm's length. Indians need to rediscover the goodness of healthy practices such as yoga and meditation.

However, there have been regional variations in occurrence of CVD which can be mapped on the basis of differing dietary pattern. For example, people from Punjab are more prone to heart diseases than people from some other regions. Also, in regions where coconut oil is used more than other oils, people have a reduced incidence of heart attacks. Coconut oil helps in increasing HDL cholesterol and, thereby, helps in improving the overall cholesterol pattern of the body. India is witnessing a demographic shift in CVD from the wealthy to the lower classes largely due to the wider availability of rich food and the advent of mass transport.

But diets and exercises are not enough to explain India's coronary calamity. One of the reasons is likely to be the gene. Even though this theory has not been fully established, I strongly believe that this might hold the key to various diseases the human race is facing. Some studies have revealed that South Asians have raised levels of artery-clogging blood chemicals, including LDL cholesterol and triglycerides. They also suffer from a deficiency of HDL cholesterol that helps clear fatty build-ups from blood vessels. More than anything else, a ratio of HDL and LDL is believed to provide an accurate account of heart condition.

South Asians are more prone to heart diseases as compared to other ethnic groups according to some recent studies. Over a period of time, South Asians adapted to frequent famines. Earlier, people were eating half meals a day or at the most one meal a day. The food was not rich and, therefore, human bodies adapted to surviving on less food. This changed in the modern world marked with an overabundance of food. Our bodies are finding it difficult to adjust to a new situation which can be described as 'a metabolic U-turn'. This has led to high insulin intolerance and accompanying problems such as raised levels of diabetes and obesity. The gene is still functioning in its own way and conserving extra fats and it may take a generation or two for the gene to adapt to the surplus food situation.

It has been found that a person with a family history of heart diseases is at a greater risk than a person who does not have a genetic tendency towards heart diseases. Therefore, such people should be more cautious and monitor their lifestyle from the very beginning. A sedentary lifestyle coupled with an atavistic tendency to heart diseases can prove disastrous for an individual. As heart diseases are increasingly infecting our younger population, people should develop a cautious attitude from the beginning.

To a large extent, most of the risks to heart can be accounted for by known risk factors such as smoking, obesity, blood pressure, unhealthy diets and lack of physical activity. Thus, it is possible to protect oneself by controlling or modifying one's lifestyle. In China, rapid economic development led to a duplication of lifestyle and resulted in an increase in the rate of CVD.

Another major cause of concern is the fact that, the number of people living below the poverty line in South Asia is quite high. This poses a problem in cases where pregnant and lactating mothers do not get proper nutritious food leading to an increase in the risk of heart diseases in foetuses. Clinical problems such as diabetes also tend to increase the risk of contracting a heart disease by a several times.

Smoking is widely accepted as the Number One risk factor for heart diseases. Nicotine raises blood pressure, damages blood vessels and multiplies the effects of cholesterol. It also worsens the fatty build-ups that directly lead to heart attacks. Smoking a single cigarette can have a measurable damaging effect on the arterial walls. Smokers continue to increase their risk of heart attack the longer they smoke. People who smoke a pack of cigarettes a day have more than twice the risk of heart attack than non-smokers.

Studies have established that women who smoke and also use oral contraceptives for birth control have several times more risk of coronary and peripheral artery diseases, heart attack and stroke than those women who do not smoke but use oral contraceptives. Smoking poses a great risk for non-smokers also. Passive smoking causes at least 35,000 deaths annually. It is not without reason that smoking is banned in public places in most developed countries and the norm is strictly adhered to by all.

Obesity is another leading culprit behind the increased vulnerability of South Asians to cardiac diseases. A recent study has claimed that South Asians tend to gain more fat around their waists than their western counterparts. Coronary heart diseases tend to claim more victims from amongst those who have high fat deposits around their waists. This puts South Asians at a greater risk than any other ethnic group.

A good diet can considerably reduce the risk of heart diseases where as a bad diet can aggravate the situation. A recent study has shown that chili and soya yoghurt can also help in lowering the incidents of cardiac problems. Prevention is always better than cure and if people are aware of simple dietary patterns that can help them keep critical situations at bay, it can go a long way in developing a healthy nation.

Milk, which is generally considered to be an irreplaceable ingredient of the Indian diet, needs to be consumed with care. Milk and milk products tend to increase the risk of heart diseases as they are rich in fats and provide rich material for arterial blockage. Therefore, everything should be taken in 'moderation' as that is the key word for a healthy living.

If drugs are given early enough and in right quantity, heart diseases may be controlled. Taking drugs to reduce cholesterol well below currently recommended levels can substantially reduce the risk of a heart attack. Stem cell research also holds great promises for treatment of CVD, but these are still early days to reach any definite conclusion. But no matter how many innovations are pioneered in the field of science and technology, we can not over look the immense potential of treatment that a heart to heart conversation engenders.

Modern technological innovations do not shift the onus of proper health care from individuals on to the doctors. Doctors are not Gods, my teacher Dr Spencer used to say and he would get very angry if doctors started believing that they were like God. I strongly believe that while a good surgery can bring a heart back to life, heart can be prevented from several ailments by practicing simple rules of good living.

A 40-45 minute walk, five-six times a week should form an indispensable part of a person's schedule. A cardiac check-up should also be an imperative part of a person's lifestyle. For men it should be undertaken after 30 years of age and for women after 40 years of age. A regular check-up can help in early identification of the risks, if any, and can make the treatment easier.

In today's world of tough competition, tougher people are the need of the hour. Human beings have had a history of social and communal living but modern lifestyle has brought all these practices to naught. Nothing works better than a heart to heart conversation with someone close and understanding. One must remember that while physical heart is an organ, the emotional heart allows human beings to feel an event. The good being of the emotional heart is significant for the well being of the organ.

Treating heart is more than a clinical job. I entirely agree with Dr Mimi that it is more than a pump. It is for cardiologists to realize this and strike a balance between being a physician and being a healer. The most difficult job is to make people develop passion for their life. She argues that emotional outbursts of anger and hostility increase the risk of a heart attack by at least 200 per cent.

Dr Mimi draws from her personal experience and tries to present heart treatment in a comprehensive way. The power of a heart to heart talk can not be duplicated in the form of any medical treatment. She underlines the fact that no matter how many innovations are made in the field of science and medicine, the basic and the most effective treatment that works wonders is an intimate talk with the patient. It is in this sense that her book *The Heart Speaks* is important in treating CVD.

Dr. Naresh Trehan *
Chief of Cardio Surgery,
Apollo Hospitals,
Delhi

---

* Naresh Trehan is the country's leading cardiologist and has performed more than 50,000 heart surgeries. He performed the first robotic heart surgery in India. He says he will not retire or rest until he has personally trained more than 100 surgeons, a human legacy that he wants to leave for his country.

Dr. Trehan has done his graduation from King George's Medical College and also holds a diplomat from American Board of Surgery and American Board of Cardiothoracic Surgery. He is the personal surgeon to the President of India and has received several prestigious national awards including Padma Shree and Padma Bhushan.

Preface

In the Western world we suffer from diseases of excess. Diabetes, high blood pressure, and high cholesterol have as their root cause poor diet, lack of exercise and maladaptive responses to stress and tension. Cardiovascular disease accounted for approximately 233,000 deaths in the UK in 2003. This staggering statistic represents one in three or 38 percent of all deaths. As of 2003 one-third of adults in the UK were inactive, exercising less than 30 minutes per week. Yet, despite these statistics, cardiovascular disease is preventable.

We now know that healing the heart truly requires a mind body spirit approach. As a young physician I was trained to focus on the physical heart. I spent many years working in the cardiac catheterization lab performing mechanical fixes with angioplasty balloons and stents. I focused on ailments of the physical body such as high blood pressure, diabetes, and high cholesterol. But one of the great privileges of medicine is that people share their lives. People often come to physicians when they are vulnerable and hurting. If you take the time to listen, they share their secret hurts, losses and desires. They share their happiness as well as their sorrow. As a young doctor I was not trained to listen to the subtle clues. In fact, most physician appointments in the United States, as in the UK, are approximately 10 minutes. Yet lessons learned from patients are shrouded in wisdom; it is from these teachers of life that I learned to listen and ask deeper questions.

Slowly, I began to realize that heart disease is not simply an illness of the physical heart. Heart disease is not simply about someone's genes. Rather, it is the story of someone's life;

their life, washing over their genes. The heart is an intricate organ, now known to secrete hormones and contain nervous tissue just like the brain. Emotional outbursts of anger and hostility increase the risk of a heart attack over 200 percent. Stress and anxiety are associated with high cardiovascular mortality. People often come to a cardiologist seeking the source of their pain, never to expect that it may be linked to their personal story. People live when, according to the medical textbooks, they should die. People die when there is no reason to live. We feel with our hearts, we love with our heart; we can die of a broken heart. In some cultures the heart is sacred, the seat of the soul. The most difficult job for a cardiologist is not picking the right medications but instilling in someone a passion for their life. The will to live and to value one's life enough to make change; to look deep and ask some painful questions.

This book is about people; those who have surrounded me on my journey. No one is put in your path by accident. Somewhere along the way I discovered that the lessons we are meant to learn, come from each other. I never expected these lessons to come from my patients.

Dr. Mimi Guarneri, 2006

About The Author

Dr. Mimi Guarneri is the founder and medical director of the Scripps Center for Integrative Medicine and is board certified in cardiology, internal medicine, nuclear medicine and holistic medicine. As an undergraduate, Dr. Guarneri was an English literature major at New York University. She received her medical degree from SUNY Medical Center in New York, where she graduated number one in her class. Dr. Guarneri trained at Cornell Medical Center, where she became assistant chief medical resident. She completed her cardiac training at New York University Medical Center and Scripps Clinic, serving as an attending physician in interventional cardiology, during which time she placed thousands of coronary stents. Recognizing the need for a more comprehensive and more holistic approach to cardiovascular disease, she pioneered the Scripps Center for Integrative Medicine where she uses state-of-the-art cardiac imaging technology and lifestyle change programs to aggressively diagnose, prevent, and treat cardiovascular disease.

She is a member of the American College of Cardiology, Alpha Omega Alpha, the American Medical Women's Association, and a Diplomat of the American Holistic Medical Association. Dr. Guarneri has authored several articles that have appeared in professional journals such as the Journal of Echocardiography and the Annals of Internal Medicine.

Biography of the Heart

The heart I learned about in medical school was a simple mechanical pump, a ten-ounce, fist-size organ that beat an average of 72 times a minute, more than 100,000 times a day. It was a four-chambered muscle, similar to those in whales and sparrows, whose sole purpose was to transport oxygenated blood to the brain and other organs.

I was trained to view the heart as a distinct, isolated organ that could be easily diagrammed and modeled in plastic, that could be regulated by a pacemaker, transplanted with a donor's, and bypassed during open-heart surgery with the help of a machine.

I was taught that while people might sing of broken or stolen or wounded hearts, in fact this hollow muscle had no relationship to the emotions, intellect, or soul.

My job as a cardiologist was to sit in my office and wait for someone to have a heart attack, then rush in and try to save him. I was trained to be a cool, heroic figure who swooped into the emergency room, found blockages, and opened them.

My role was technical; my tools were catheters and stents, plastic and stainless steel. In the cath lab, where I spent most of my early doctoring years, I worked on patients in the most intimate way possible—on their living, beating hearts—yet they were in a large sense invisible to me. They passed by, a blur of indistinct faces, with lives I rarely had the time to consider. I spent my days propping open their arteries with metal sleeves called stents, without considering why they had closed in the first place.

I was taught that other parts of my patient's body were for different specialists to manage. Renal, pulmonary, and neuro doctors all had their own regions of expertise.

The mind and spirit were no one's territory. Ministers, psychologists, massage therapists—professionals in the outside world—would be the ones to deal with whatever trauma, heartache, grief, or other emotions plagued my heart patients.

No one spoke of the other layers of the heart that didn't appear on a stress test or electrocardiogram: the mental heart, affected by hostility, stress, and depression, the emotional heart that could be crushed by loss, the intelligent heart that has a nervous system of its own and communicates with the brain and other parts of the body. No one lectured about the spiritual heart that yearns for a higher purpose, the universal heart that communicates with others, or the original heart that beats in the unborn foetus before the brain is formed.

Yet other cultures and spiritual traditions have shared more complex views about the nature of the heart. The Greeks believed the spirit resided in the heart. In traditional Chinese medicine, the heart is believed to store the spirit, shen. The idea of the heart as an inner book, which contains a record of a person's entire life—emotions, ideas, and memories—appears in early Christian theology, but may have ancient roots that go back to Egyptian culture.

No other part of the human body has been so widely commemorated in poetry, so commonly used as a symbol for love and the soul, so frequently appropriated for religious purposes. The heart shows up in ancient stained-glass windows, on Victorian valentine boxes, in Shakespearean sonnets, and in a thousand love songs.

Yet from an early age, I knew that the human heart held our deepest powers and secrets. Heart disease, with its layers of grief and guilt, stress and love, had blasted a hole through the center of my own family.

On an evening when I was eight-years-old, my vivacious forty-year-old mother told me she had pain in her chest, then got into bed and died of a heart attack. That my mother—so young and alive—could simply cease to be was a defining event for me, the shock of my young life. My father's subsequent death from heart disease at fifty, almost a decade later, was surely hastened by this tragedy in our family.

Part of the reason I became a heart doctor was to overcome the powerlessness I felt as a young girl that night in Brooklyn when my mother was taken from me. Perhaps by becoming a cardiologist, I was trying in some symbolic way to reach back in time and heal the hearts in the middle of my family that had stopped beating far too soon.

This book, then, is the story of how I was trained to see the heart as a simple mechanical pump and was led by my patients to appreciate it as a center of great complexity and power.

I view the heart now as a flower, one exquisite layer opening to the next. It is to this large, multilayered heart of feeling and poetry, intelligence and spirit that I have dedicated my life.

Listening to the Heart

It is difficult for most of us to imagine the heart, since until recently, it's been impossible to actually see.

We're more familiar with the functioning of our laptops, the operating instructions for our DVDs, than we are with this powerhouse, pounding in the center of our chests. In fact, we rarely even consider the heart unless a doctor warns us that it's weak or sick or about to fail.

This may be why the sudden sight of her heart on an echocardiogram monitor made my patient, a buttoned-down accountant, burst into tears: "There's my heart! Oh God, look at it!" she exclaimed, as if she were coming face-to-face with an unexpected wonder or marvel, which indeed she was.

Through imaging technology such as echocardiograms, it is now possible to view what was previously left to dry academic description or floating formaldehyde specimens—our own living, beating hearts.

Yet the total heart in all its complexity and power cannot ever be fully fathomed by simply looking at a screen.

Clearly perceiving the heart involves more than studying an echocardiogram; listening to it requires more than a stethoscope.

Each heart has its own biography, language, and method of revealing its truth, if we know how to listen.

In *The Heart Speaks*, I will explore what patients have revealed to me about the true nature of this multilayered and complex organ by sharing their stories and their lives as well as the new science that puts the heart at the center of our intelligence, decision-making power, and memory.

Acknowledgments

As I walk into the waiting room at the Scripps Center for Integrative Medicine, I am reminded of what a privilege it is to be a physician. People come to us in their most open and vulnerable state. Our role as physicians, nurses, and healers is to serve and be of service. I thank all of those people who have come into my life and have shared their lives with me. Throughout the ages, telling stories has been a way to pass down gifts from one generation to the next, a ritual of memories and tradition. Teaching through stories, whether at the Passover table or in the waiting room, is a way to connect; it reminds us of our bonds as human beings. The telling of my story and the stories of my patients would not have been possible without three women—Janis Vallely, Lynn Lauber, and Nancy Hancock—who decided that stories from the heart and about the heart were worth recording. To them I am truly grateful.

Part I
The Myth of
the Mechanical Pump

Chapter One

The Unexamined Heart

In my work at the Scripps Center for Integrative Medicine in La Jolla, California, we teach a technique called guided imagery, in which patients are asked to visualize goals for their future lives. But when I was a girl this was called daydreaming, and I did it on my own.

Sitting on the stoop of my grandmother's brownstone apartment house in Bensonhurst, Brooklyn, where my father, brothers, and I lived after my mother's death, I watched Mrs. Puleo pushing her colicky twins under the elevated subway to the park; I saw Mrs. Calmino leading her husband home after a night of drinking; and I imagined another kind of life for myself—where I wouldn't be known for my homemade sausage or crocheted doilies, where I wouldn't be waiting at a window, darning someone else's socks.

Even as a child, I was a triple type A personality. I wanted to kick the ball down the street as high as the boys did; I wanted to be the first in my class to read. I wanted to grow into the kind of woman I'd never known but had read about in books—an updated version of Marie Curie, brave in her radium lab, being unwittingly poisoned by the very substance she discovered.

I envisioned my sovereign self in the center of an elaborate future—where I'd have a house of my own with a pool and be engaged in valiant work that would help improve the world. This was the future I was imagining as I sat on the stoop in Brooklyn. As a girl, I needed this steaming, stifling neighborhood, where everyone knew your business, where the whole street smelled of marinara sauce on Wednesday nights and fried fish on Fridays.

Growing up in the tight-knit, insular world of Brooklyn in the early sixties, I felt as if I were dangling my foot in another century. Italian immigrants and their descendants populated my neighbourhood. Climbing roses and backyard grape arbours, lacy Communion dresses and social clubs—in these and other ways, our community was as traditional and family centered as the Italian villages they'd left behind.

With my olive skin and dark hair, I could have stepped out of a sepia photograph of these turn-of-the-century immigrants. I was Italian on both sides of my family, as pure as the olive oil that my grandmother stocked in our family store.

The safe predictability of Bensonhurst was a comfort after my mother's death from a *myocardial infarction*. When I looked this up in our dictionary, it read: "the death of heart muscle from the sudden blockage of a coronary artery by a blood clot." But I still couldn't understand how this could happen.

At night I pressed my hand over my own heart to calm my fears that it might suddenly stop. I was amazed that I could actually *feel* my heart, a perpetual drumbeat keeping me alive, unlike my brain or liver.

I became fascinated with hearts, studying the red plastic anatomical model that sat in the back of my science class, that could be taken apart, showing mysterious chambers, vessels, and valves.

In the middle of my Sunday-school book, I scrutinized a depiction of the Virgin Mary, in her rose-coloured dress and blue veil, pointing to her own heart, swollen and surrounded by rays of light, as if she were trying to convey a potent secret.

I studied *The Sacred Heart of Jesus*, a print that hung in a position of prominence in my grandmother's bedroom: Jesus stood in a white robe, his red heart full of wounds, surrounded by a crown of thorns and a burning fire.

But nothing I saw or read squared in my mind the demise of my own mother, whose heart attack sat in the center of my childhood, a calamity of mythic proportions that was never discussed.

That I had been with her when she died linked us even further, though what lodged in me was the bitter fact that I'd been too young to save her.

I took solace in the family that remained, all stacked in my grandmother's building, each black-lacquered door opening into a singular, intimate world. No matter what I needed, there was always a haven. If I was hungry,

I was handed a plate of pasta from the hot second-floor kitchen of my aunt Rose. When I felt lonely, I opened the door to my cousin Joann's bedroom for a blaring initiation into Janis Joplin and the Grateful Dead. And when I needed advice or protection, I tucked myself into that warren of heat and thwarted ambition, my grandmother's apartment.

Short and fierce, her hands strong as a mechanic's, my grandmother was the matriarch not only of our family but also of the neighbourhood, and the one who ran our small family grocery store.

I grew up as her protégée and project, waiting on customers, slicing salami, stocking shelves. I can still see the blue boxes of macaroni and the red cans of condensed milk and feel the coolness of the marble counters on my arms in summer. By her silent example, she taught me a dozen lessons of service and charity, the chief of them being: The customer always comes first.

This wasn't just sales talk; she meant that you had to take care of people around you before you concerned yourself with profit. When our next-door neighbour Mr. Rico woke us in the middle of the night because his boy was sick, my grandmother heaved herself from bed, her long braid trailing down her back, and maneuvered down the steep stairs to open the store and get him a quart of milk. She walked through rain to deliver rations to bedridden Mrs. Riley; she always scraped up quarters to loan from the bottom of her big black purse.

She had imported more from Italy than the plum tomatoes and Romano cheese we sold at the store. She'd also brought with her old-world ways I loved—peasant meals of beans and pasta, a backyard garden of basil and arugula, our family suppers and after-dinner walks.

In our neighbourhood, everyone felt bound together—they understood who they were and where they belonged. This communal atmosphere infused me with a feeling of safety and connection; the sense of community was a great environment for the heart.

Of course, there was also a dark side to all that predictability and conformity. If you were an outsider, like the African-American family who haplessly migrated onto our block one summer, you were treated to scalding bigotry and excluded from the fold.

And the barriers hemming in women weren't visible, but they were as sharp as wire: After graduation, girls like me were still expected to find a local boy and settle down to a domestic life that would be dominated by raising children. Down the street or up the block, that was how far most girls in my neighbourhood got—no farther than their mothers.

But this wasn't for me. My mother had lived long enough to instill in me the value of independence, and my grandmother had created an environment that allowed me to thrive.

"Make sure you've got your own, Mimi," my mother used to say when she cooked my breakfast. "When you're independent, you don't owe anyone. You can always take care of yourself."

I tucked this away for later consumption; I knew that as much as I needed this neighborhood now, someday I'd also need to leave it.

Unbeknownst to me, at the same time I was growing up in Bensonhurst, a similar world of Italian immigrants was being studied for their extraordinary lack of heart disease. Dr. Stewart Wolf, a physician, and John G. Bruhn, a sociologist, had embarked on a long-term study of the inhabitants of Roseto, Pennsylvania, from 1935 through 1984.[1]

Despite the community's smoking, eating a fatty diet, and spending their days in the hazardous labour of slate quarries, the citizens of Roseto, the researchers discovered, appeared to be almost immune to heart disease, dying at a rate only half that of the rest of the country.

Roseto's early Italian immigrants had built their own culture of cooperation after being ostracized by the Welsh and English, who'd once dominated their small area of eastern Pennsylvania. They created a kind of civic spirit, celebrating religious festivals and family occasions together, evolving into an intensely connected community.

In Roseto, as in Bensonhurst, neighbors looked after one another, generations lived together under a single roof, and the elderly were included as part of a close-knit web. Church festivals, social clubs, and family dinners brought people together and served to ward off isolation and loneliness.

Through the 1960s, Roseto was characterized by stability, predictability, and conformity. Families lived in small homes on tightly packed streets; neighbours often filled one another's kitchens after dinner. Since any display of wealth was discouraged, the distance between rich and poor was diminished. The work ethic was paramount: A common goal shared by nearly everyone was a better future for their children.

In the end, the researchers decided that the Roseto Effect on heart disease was caused by something that couldn't be measured in a lab—social networks, civic interconnectedness, stability, and predictability.

"People are nourished by other people," said Wolf, noting that the characteristics of tight-knit community were better predictors of healthy hearts than cholesterol levels or smoking.[2]

Many studies have corroborated the powerful effect that social and cultural factors play in health and cardiovascular functioning. The "biophilia" hypothesis—that living things yearn for proximity to other living things—translates, in the case of humans, to the fact that most of us of us are happiest and healthiest around others.[3] For much of history, humans have lived together in intimate groups, banding together as a matter of survival. Now many of us live spread out and cut off, without the leagues, guilds, and clubs that once gave us a sense of connection to our communities.

In studies conducted in Alameda County, California, and North Karelia, Finland, thousands of participants were observed for five to nine years. Compared with participants who felt most connected to others, socially isolated participants demonstrated a two to threefold increased risk of death from heart disease and all other causes. Strikingly, these results were independent of other cardiac risk factors.[4, 5]

In the beta-blocker heart attack trial reported in *The New England Journal of Medicine*, male heart attack survivors who were socially isolated and had a high degree of life stress had more than four times the risk of death from heart disease and other causes than men who reported low levels of isolation and stress.[6] And a study of more than four thousand men of Japanese ancestry living in Hawaii found that social networks were protective against coronary artery disease during a seven year period. This protection was independent of known health hazards such as high blood pressure and cigarette smoking.[7]

The researchers studying Roseto predicted that younger community members would not remain satisfied with the traditional values of their parents, and they were correct. As the next generation grew up and went to college, they became less concerned with Roseto's communal way of life and more focused on material success. They began to show off their wealth by buying larger cars and single-family homes on the outskirts of town.

When the researchers returned in the 1970s, they found a changing landscape—the close-knit community that had been heart-protective was rapidly disappearing. Young professionals were driving their cars out of the community for sedentary white-collar jobs. They fenced in their yards and grew more self-centered, retreating into their nuclear families instead of focusing on the larger clan.

Wolf and his colleagues discovered that the village's social changes were accompanied by increased health problems. By the seventies, Roseto's resistance to heart disease had been reversed, and the first heart attack of a person younger than forty-five occurred in 1971. The rate of heart disease continued to rise until it eventually reached the national average. The town had lost its statistical uniqueness. The golden age of Roseto had passed.

And in our own little microcosm of Bensonhurst, we followed suit. The changes that Roseto began seeing were also ones that began affecting us.

On our street, increased prosperity meant less walking and a congestion of Chevys and Buicks; pasta was replaced by my father's new favorite dinner, sirloin and blue cheese. Backyards were fenced in with chain-link and picket; commuters left the neighbourhood for suburban jobs. Old Mrs. Esposito and Mr. Como disappeared from the upstairs bedrooms of their children's houses into nursing homes.

Eventually, an appliance store appeared on the corner of Thirteenth Avenue, replacing Falcones', the newspaper and candy store that had been a neighborhood meeting place for years. Falcones' was where you went if you lost your key or were looking for your father, or if you were simply lonely and wanted to stand amid the gossip before heading back out into the cooler, more anonymous world.

After forty years at the same spot, the Falcones vanished, back to Italy, some said. Taking their place behind the plate glass were cool white washing machines, dishwashers, vacuum cleaners, and air conditioners.

"Where will everyone go when they need to talk?" I asked my aunt Rose, but she only shrugged and shook her head.

If my great-grandparents from Calabria had suddenly materialized in our apartment, dragging their farm instruments behind them, they would have been shocked by how technology, automation, and leisure began transforming life during the sixties. They would have been amazed at how much time we spent slumped in front of the TV as our clothes and dishes were automatically washed. They would have been dismayed by how isolated and sedentary we'd become.

We've lost track of the sheer physicality and interdependence that characterized life up until our century—the bread baking, butter churning, fire tending, rug beating. A household task as simple as laundry once was a daylong labour, involving scrubbing, wringing, hanging—all weight-bearing, cardiac-stimulating work.

The average person lives an extraordinarily easy life compared with that of our forebears—driving a car even short distances; taking elevators instead of climbing stairs; regularly eating butter, ice cream, cheese, and other rich foods that once were luxuries, made by hand. Seven out of ten of us are not involved in physical exercise *of any kind*. In fact, the typical modern person is now involved in exertion—at home or work—only half as many hours as in the nineteenth century.[8]

That the average worker now earns his or her living without ceaseless physical toil is certainly an accomplishment. It's hard to romanticize the days when a woman spent all day washing bedclothes by hand and lugging them out to dry.

Before 1900, cardiovascular disease was relatively rare; people were more likely to die from pneumonia, influenza, or tuberculosis. The life expectancy of the typical American has nearly doubled—from a little over forty at the beginning of the twentieth century to seventy-seven at the start of the twenty-first. While it is definitely a positive development that life is becoming steadily longer, these increased years have often been accompanied by chronic disability and illness. Cardiovascular disease is the leader of the list, the prime killer in the United States, claiming more lives than the rest of major causes of death.[9]

Meanwhile, in my own private world, my father, Joseph, was a silent addition to these terrible statistics. He died of a heart attack, nearly a decade after my mother, leaving our surviving family as baffled in the face of this mysterious disease as we'd been before.

My grandmother, born in the 1890s, was the last of the old-world clan in Bensonhurst. She was the last of the peach pickers, the noodle makers, the elders who knew the middle name of every child on the block.

By the time of her final illness, however, technology had not only swept through our neighborhood but had also pervaded the world of medicine. Hearts that stopped beating could be shocked alive with defibrillators. Ventilators pushed air and oxygen into exhausted lungs. Artificial hydration extended life in those who could no longer eat, but it also prolonged their dying. Instead of patients being surrounded at home by friends and family, it was not uncommon for them to end up alone in a sterile hospital room.

My grandmother wanted none of these life-extending procedures. She may not have understood the technical facts of her congestive heart failure—that her narrowing aortic valve was causing her heart to overwork, creating fluid retention and stiffness of her heart muscle—but she felt the *emotional* truth of it. She knew her heart was gradually wearing down like an old, faltering clock.

"I don't want to die in a hospital." This was the refrain of my grandmother, who, like most of us, wanted to remain in her apartment and spend her final days in peace, not in a room choked with beeping monitors and IVs.

But the availability of these new procedures created medical dilemmas for my family that our ancestors had never had to contemplate. How could my grandmother simply be left in her apartment when there was technology at the medical center that might prolong her life? Like so many families in this situation, we succumbed.

She was checked in to the hospital, entering a clinical system where symptoms were treated because they could be, because they were *there*.

But my ancient Italian grandmother knew better than the young technicians with their ventilators and medications that there was nothing they could do for her. And she was right.

She was smarter than us all.

"Everything's changed!" my grandmother used to exclaim to me about the near century she had witnessed. And it was true—what *hadn't* been invented during the last hundred years?

Standing at the kitchen sink peeling potatoes, she used to tick off the advances—moon travel, zippers, atom bombs, antibiotics, computers, Scotch tape.

But behind these advances were other changes that were harder to tally—the anonymity and isolation, the loss of community right outside our Brooklyn blinds.

Most of us realized how these changes affected the way we lived, without considering how profoundly they might also affect the way we would die.

Chapter Two

A Heart, a Spleen,
a Leaking Valve

In my position as a cardiologist, it has taken me a long time to have an open heart.

The process of becoming as physician is like being initiated into a secret society—a subculture with its own language, code, and hierarchy, one that doesn't allow you to show your emotions.

They don't tell you this, but they teach it to you.

My training started the first day of medical school, in anatomy class, with fifty of us initiates crowded into a lab.

Bright lights, white walls, the sweet scent of formaldehyde. And there in front of us: rows of dead bodies covered up on slabs.

The professor was standing in front of us talking about dissecting procedures, but I wasn't paying attention, not really. All I could think about were those bodies, lying there—someone's grandmother, father, wife.

I especially dreaded pulling back the sheet and peering down at those faces, seeing the pierced ears, the curls, the furrows, the particularities that made up a person.

My dissection partner, Carol, and I were assigned to a large-boned woman with a brown page boy threaded with gray.

When it was time to begin our procedure, I drew back the sheet and we both stood there speechless, staring down at the nails still painted coral, the plucked eyebrows, the worn spot on the left-hand finger where a wedding band must have been.

"God, I can't work on this woman," Carol whispered.

"Why not?"

"She looks just like my mom."

I turned my gaze to Carol; she had grown nearly as pale as our corpse.

"Okay, I'll cut, and you read the instructions."

Carol blew out a breath and opened the manual. "We're going to start with her carotid artery."

I covered the woman's face again and took out my scalpel.

And so it began. That's how we made it through.

Like car mechanics, we narrowed and fragmented, zeroed in on an arm, a spleen, a heart valve, so that the woman in front of us gradually disappeared and became a compilation of parts.

After weeks of dissection, we'd cut and sliced so much that we nearly forgot that the flesh we were handling had once been a breathing human body.

One day I entered the class as a male classmate ambled across the room with someone's leg flung over his shoulder, and it didn't even faze me. It had happened—I'd entered another realm.

It was not only medical school that taught me to shut down my emotions; many patients even seemed to expect it.

When I was an intern at Cornell in internal medicine, I was taking care of a woman named Ann, who was in her thirties and suffering from leukemia. She was a real trouper, feisty and full of spunk. She and her husband were one of those couples who united under adversity. It seemed to me they were always there, huddled together over a crossword puzzle in the corridor whenever I began my rounds. I'd watched Ann's diminishment over the months with a kind of terrible awe; first she lost her mass of red wavy hair, then her fresh complexion, then even her eyebrows. But rather than dwell on their losses, she somehow kept upbeat and focused.

"Dr. Mimi, can you think of a six-letter word for *seer*?" she asked one day when I was drawing her blood.

"Nope, you're the brain."

She was dressed again and out in the hall when I heard her cry out, "*Oracle*! I got it!"

I couldn't imagine where she found her fortitude.

Finally, after she'd struggled through grueling stretches of chemotherapy, there was a spot of light, the long-hoped-for breakthrough. Ann's tests were clear; she'd gone into remission. Her next stop was Sloan-Kettering for a bone-marrow transplant.

I felt a great surge of relief the day I watched Ann walk out of the Cornell lobby, slender as a heron, with her blue dress and bald head, her arm hooked through her husband's. This was why I was becoming a doctor, I said to myself. This was the miracle of modern medicine.

Ann returned home to great fanfare. According to accounts I gleaned from the nurses' station, her family threw parties that weekend, and relatives came from all over the country to celebrate her return. Gradually, she slipped off my radar screen, replaced by the never-ending line of other pressing patients.

So I was surprised a few weeks later when I ran into her husband up on the floor.

"What are you doing here? I thought Ann was headed to Sloan-Kettering."

Her husband avoided my eyes and attached his gaze to a spot down the hall. He looked weary, with a stubbled beard. "Ann started talking strangely last week—a kind of babbling —so we brought her in again."

I tried to keep my face from showing what I'd immediately surmised—that the cancer had most likely traveled to Ann's brain.

Later that evening I steeled myself and walked into the room to see her.

"Hey, Ann," I said, touching her slender arm. She looked up at me oddly, with a squint, as if she weren't sure who—or even what—I was. There had been massive deterioration in the weeks since I'd seen her. She had great difficulty focusing on our conversation, and her eyes wandered around the room. Her husband, sitting by her side, attempted to orient her, but it was nearly impossible.

I tried my best to continue my banter, to remain upbeat and cheerful, but seeing her like this when we had all had such hope, I felt something slip from under me.

My face began that wobbly tremor that was a precursor to tears. Then, sure enough, tears filled my eyes. I patted Ann's hand and walked quickly out into the corridor.

Her husband was on my heels, furious. "That was completely unprofessional, showing your emotions like that," he said. "It's telling her there's no hope."

It was one thing to have a colleague tell me to toughen up; it was quite another hearing it from a patient's husband.

It was a terrible lesson, one I took to heart. *I simply can't reveal my feelings.*

In some deep part of myself, I reinforced the brick wall that was already surrounding my emotions.

During all my years of training, only one voice dissented from this view of cool, clinical detachment: an elderly doctor whom I encountered during professor rounds when I was interning at Cornell.

Silver-haired and stooped, stethoscopes and reflex hammers stuffed in his pocket, he looked like a relic from another century.

I was brash and arrogant, having just graduated number one in my medical-school class. Watching him, I found myself thinking: *I know all the latest techniques. What's this old geezer going to teach me?*

Still, the other interns and I followed him down the hall as he lingered over patients, telling lame jokes and listening to their long-winded anecdotes.

I kept looking at my watch, eager to end my rounds so I could rush off to more important tasks—lab results, admission reports, and charting—but the old doctor wouldn't be hurried.

When he finally finished with the last patient, he took off his glasses and peered solemnly at us.

"There's one thing I want to tell you before I leave today, a lesson you won't learn in medical school. If you let patients speak and tell their stories, and you really listen, they'll give you their diagnosis. But if you keep interrupting them and they don't get to tell it, you'll keep ordering tests and lab work and you'll miss the answer that's right in front of you."

I filed away this advice with everything else that was jammed in my mind—medication dosages, warning signs for heart failure, liver disease, and hepatitis, and the pained, anxious looks on the faces under my care. While I felt the old doctor's advice was right, who actually had the time?

During my decade of training I was so physically exhausted, so sleep deprived and stressed, that I often felt as if I were seasick or drunk, moving through a never-ending dream.

I staggered through the days desperate to keep everything straight and not make a vital error. I was immersed in the minutiae, the drama and intimacy of strangers' lives and bodies —their breasts and feet, their moles and glands, their mysterious blood counts, coughs, and swellings.

Yet even in the midst of the fatigue and stress, I kept coming back to that old doctor's words.

In medical school, I liked to chat with an affable, middleaged African-American truck driver named Mr. Washington who'd been diagnosed with Lou Gehrig's disease and was paralyzed from the neck down.

Given the terrible, fatal progression of Lou Gehrig's, Mr. Washington was considered a closed case. The consensus was that he was finished, so no one wasted much time on him.

He was entirely frozen except for his big, handsome head and his expressive eyes, in which, it seemed to me, he concentrated the force of all he was.

Whenever I stopped in to take his vitals, he turned his moist gaze my way and I couldn't resist listening to him chat about his wife's sweet-potato pie or his boxing career in high school.

One day he told me, "You know, nobody ever listens when I say this, but I was fine before my accident."

"What accident?"

"My truck accident. I got hit from behind a couple of months ago. When I was checked out at the ER, the docs told me I was fine—maybe a little whiplash. Then boom—only a few weeks after that I couldn't move. I think my problem has something to do with that accident."

I looked at his chart—the accident was noted with other portions of his history, but no one had questioned whether it was relevant to his diagnosis.

"And you mentioned this to the other doctors?"

"Yeah, I tried to, but nobody paid any attention."

"Okay," I told him. "Let me look into it."

My attending was a neurologist, well known for his arrogant brusqueness.

I entered his office and found him reviewing cases. He looked up at me with clear annoyance. "Yes?"

"I was just talking to Washington in 603. He tells me that he was fine until he hurt his neck in a truck accident. I was wondering if we could get a CT scan and take a look."

The doctor took off his glasses, the better to intimidate me. "Mr. W. has Lou Gehrig's disease. That's his diagnosis. He's going to die of it. This has nothing to do with his neck or any accident."

And with that, I was dismissed.

But I couldn't get Mr. Washington out of my mind. I was on call that night, and every time I walked by his room, I caught sight of him, lying there alone, looking up at the ceiling. *What if he's right?* I asked myself. *What if there's even the tiniest chance he's right? Isn't it worth investigating?*

My grandmother's voice floated back to me from the storage room of our old family grocery. *Mimi, the customer always comes first!*

If Mr. Washington wasn't my customer, who was?

I went to find my chief resident, who was sitting blearily over a pile of charts.

"Listen, I think Mr. Washington may have a disc in his neck that's causing his paralysis instead of Lou Gehrig's disease, but Dr. J. says I'm not allowed to scan his neck."

He didn't even look up at me. "So?"

"So I need your help. We could take him down right now and get him scanned ourselves."

I'd watched this resident with patients, so I knew he was a good guy. But he realized as well as I did that I was only a medical student and butting heads with the attending was a risky thing for me to do.

"Let me see the file," he said.

I watched him shuffle through the papers, stopping to read certain test results. Finally, he closed it and let out a sigh.

"Okay. But you could be getting me fired and yourself thrown out of medical school."

"That won't happen," I said, but it was sheer bravado.

At 2 A.M., we rolled a gurney into Mr. Washington's room. Even though it was two in the morning, he was awake, almost as if he expected us. He turned his head my way when we transferred him onto the gurney.

I whispered: "We're going to get you checked out, Mr. Washington. But we've got to be quiet."

I was terrified as we wheeled him down the hall toward the CT-scan room. I half expected the attending or one of his minions to spring from a darkened office and nab us, but we were lucky.

After Mr. W.'s neck was scanned, the chief resident and I studied the results. Just as I'd suspected, there was a disc pushing on his spinal cord.

The resident smiled, in spite of himself. "Man, look at that! You were right."

The next morning a group of us, led by the attending neurologist, made patient rounds, then X-ray rounds.

One by one, each patient's X-rays were illuminated and reviewed.

I'd added Mr. Washington's at the very end, without telling the attending. Finally, it flashed on the screen.

"What's this?" the attending asked.

I said, "Doctor, that's Mr. Washington. We went ahead and scanned his neck, and as you can see, there's a disc impinging on his spinal cord."

The doctor stood facing the X-ray for a long moment, and I could see a muscle working in his jaw. I looked over at the chief resident, who'd gone pale.

"Go get the surgeon," the attending finally said gruffly, turning on his heel. "That's it for today."

Several weeks later, I'd just finished drawing blood from an elderly woman when the chief resident walked by and stopped at a window facing the parking lot.

"Mimi, come and look at this."

I walked over to him and looked out the grimy window. A stocky woman in a winter coat was pushing an African-American man through the parking lot to a battered-looking station wagon: It was Mr. Washington. When the woman reached the car, she left him on the passenger's side and went around to open the trunk.

My beeper buzzed in my pocket, and I put my hand in and shut it off without even looking. I realized I was barely breathing. When the women came back to Mr. Washington, she gave him an arm and Mr. Washington hoisted his girth out of the wheelchair and stood.

"Mimi, they need you down in Room 112, stat," a nurse called behind me. As I turned, the resident reached out and squeezed my arm.

"Always listen to the patient," I said as I moved down the hall.

Across space and time, my old professor had saved another life.

Kings County Hospital, where I met Mr. Washington, was like nowhere else in the world; situated in East New York, it was a war zone in the middle of a third-world country. When I was there in the eighties, there were still windowless tuberculosis wards.

The emergency room was a hellish scene of human malfunction—a United Nations of suffering. A swarm of languages—Spanish, patois, Cantonese—could be heard through the halls. It was hard to take in the staggering number of ways a human body could be damaged—the concussions, contusions, and overdoses, the slashings from penknives, ice picks, box cutters, the awful dailiness of gunshot wounds.

At posh medical schools, a student would barely touch a patient, but instead would stand at the end of the bed and watch, her hands still and clean. But city hospitals like Kings County were so desperate for help that I was pulled by my collar straight into the fray.

The good news was that this was the best training I could ever have found. The bad news was that I got tossed in, head-first, and had to figure it out frequently on my own.

There's a saying at the city hospitals: *See one, do one, teach one.*

My first day on an ob-gyn rotation, I walked over to the chief resident, a harried-looking woman in her twenties with two pairs of eyeglasses and multiple prescription pads stuffed in her pocket, and introduced myself.

"Hook those women up to the power line," she said, motioning to the hallway outside.

Luckily, I knew what she was referring to—IVs of Pitocin, a drug in common use at that time to accelerate childbirth.

But I blanched when I turned the corner and found gurney after gurney of women in various stages of dilation, all speaking the universal language of advanced labour: heart rending moans and wails.

I'd never put in an IV before, but pregnant women supposedly had big, fat veins that were easy to access.

I approached my first patient, a young Hispanic woman with panicked eyes and a stomach stretched taut as a tawny balloon.

"Have you ever had a baby?" she asked me in a wild voice, gripping on to my hand like a vise.

"No, I haven't," I said, sizing up her right arm for veins.

She squeezed my hand even harder as a new contraction passed over her. "Well, don't!" she screamed out, arching her back and almost pulling me down on top of her.

I was able to insert her IV on the second try, but others were more challenging. By the time I had reached the end of the line, I was covered with blood, but there was this: I knew how to insert IVs for the rest of my life.

From the heart perspective, I saw arcane diseases such as mitral stenosis, a narrowing of the valve on the left side of the heart. This was a condition rarely seen in the United States but common in patients from third-world countries. If strep throat wasn't treated by antibiotics, patients often contracted rheumatic fever, which then damaged the heart's mitral valve, and sometimes the aortic valve as well.

Then there were the junkies who had contracted endocarditis —an infection of the heart valves—from years of shooting heroin.

Their veins were so tapped and collapsed from injecting drugs that I often spent hours trying to locate one strong enough to insert an IV line.

One Saturday, I tried all afternoon to insert an IV in Benny, a once-dapper ladies' man and heroin addict, who was regularly admitted for his declining health. He was in bad shape, coming down from a high, and he was belligerent— spitting and cursing me. "You bitch! Get out of here! Stop hurting me!"

"I see Benny's being charming again today," my friend Sue said as she passed by.

I looked up at her. "You want to take over?"

"No thanks," she sang out as she passed by. "I have to see the jail guys," referring to inmates of the hospital's prison ward, who were mysteriously stricken with dire illness whenever female physicians were on call.

By the time I finally got the IV into Benny and started his medication, I was exhausted. My neck hurt from craning over him, I hadn't had lunch, and there was a sick, unhappy crowd of patients ahead of me.

I took a break and ran upstairs to take a shower and grab a snack from the hospital vending machines. On the way back down, half an hour later, I passed Benny's room, then backed up and did a double take: A small crowd of his friends were clustered around him, smiling broadly, one with his hand on the IV pole. Benny, who had been writhing and swearing all day, was now draped back against his pillow, a beatific smile on his face, one silver tooth glinting like a dime.

"What are you doing!" I yelled as I walked into the room, though I'd already figured it out: Benny's friends had helped out their friend by shooting heroin into his IV line.

I faced more hours finding a new vein for another IV, though Benny was considerably more sedate the second time around.

At the city hospital we also had to contend with the exodus of a whole generation of beautiful young men, stricken in the early days of AIDS. They weren't in individual rooms, with privacy and special care, but were dying together in large dormitory-like wards, lined up in one terrible row after another, some on ventilators, others perched for hours on bedpans with AIDS-related diarrhoea no one knew how to treat.

I was the resident, with two female interns beneath me, and the three of us were responsible for the entire ward. They called us Charlie's Angels because all we did was dash from room to room trying to put out fires.

As a result of the immunosuppressive effects of AIDS, we came across obscure opportunistic infections we never thought we'd face in a lifetime—pneumocystis carinii, cryptosporidium, and rare forms of tuberculosis.

And the flow of new patients was never ending.

That was the worst: being on call in the emergency room when another healthy-looking young man came in whose main symptom was shortness of breath.

"Are you breathless when you exert yourself or all the time?" I asked, listening to the lungs of a nineteen-year-old with a thatch of hay-colored hair.

"All the time," he said gravely.

"Okay, I'm going to run a few tests and we'll see what we've got here," although the terrible confluence of facts had already rung a bell, one that had been rung too many times: young man, shortness of breath, weight loss.

Sure enough, when I looked at his sputum under the microscope, I could see the diagnosis already being typed into the official hospital records: another case of pneumocystis carinii.

Then I had to steel myself to walk back into the room and tell this young man that he had AIDS; at that time treatment was minimal, and it was likely he would die.

I was eventually so drained by the city hospital that I switched to Cornell, an alternate universe on the other side of town—patients arriving with their belongings in Gucci totes instead of shopping bags. Prominent gay men stricken with AIDS, as doomed as their counterparts across town, were tucked away in rooms with splendid views of the East River.

On the wards I was surrounded by harried residents from Yale and Harvard who were still frantically running around trying to figure out how to draw blood when I had long finished with my patients. My training at Kings County Hospital might have been exhausting, but it had taught me well.

For nearly a decade, I virtually lived inside the sheltered world of hospitals, with their special climate and buzzing fluorescence, their drifting scents of blood and cafeteria beef. I was a creature of labs, attuned to beeps and lights, giving myself up to only the thinnest crust of sleep.

By the time I became assistant chief resident at Cornell, I'd evolved into a tough, lean clinical machine.

One evening, a younger male colleague put his head down on the desk and started weeping when I asked him to do an admission in the middle of the night.

"I'm too exhausted to do another admission! I've got to eat. I can barely stand up."

On our ward at that moment a woman was dying of lung cancer, a man was in kidney failure, and a teenager had somehow contracted a combination of mononucleosis and hepatitis B.

I didn't have two minutes in my schedule for this guy's weakness; in fact, I found myself repulsed by his vulnerability.

"Get your act together; you have to do it." I turned on my heel and walked out.

It didn't take long before I heard his rubber-soled shoes squenching up behind me.

"Who's first?"

"Mrs. Curtis, in 317. Get an ECG, then call gastro to set up a consult."

After a moment I heard my colleague call out behind me, "I think she wants to talk to someone about her diagnosis . . ."

But I was already halfway down the hall, reviewing the results of a spinal tap, picking up a page, trying to figure out why the guy in the next room was still yowling in pain when he was on a morphine drip. All my fine intentions were pushed aside; I had become a soldier, operating in survival mode, under a cloud of exhaustion.

"Later," I said.

Part II
The Language
of the Heart

Chapter Three

The Fog of Stress

Whenever I'm asked whether stress can actually cause a heart attack, I think of Paul. When Paul became my patient, I had already completed my cardiac fellowship and moved to San Diego, not for the beaches or the weather but for the cardiac catheterization lab at Scripps Clinic in La Jolla, where the coronary stent was pioneered. I wanted to be a part of these modern marvels that could alter a patient's life in minutes. By inserting one of these metal sleeves into a blocked artery, a patient's chest pain could be alleviated and he could return home within a day. The success of this procedure was so revolutionary that I accepted an advanced fellowship to learn coronary stenting from the pros.

Not that I minded taking a break from New York's brutal winters and humid summers, its trash and high rents. But I believed that I'd be back to New York after a year's break, and in that I was wrong. I found Scripps Clinic progressive and exciting and La Jolla a revelation after the cement landscape of New York. Light and water, gold and blue, sparkled in my peripheral vision. Gradually, it dawned on me that I could actually *choose* to stay on in this balmy place.

By the time my fellowship drew to a close, the gravitational pull back east that I'd initially felt had vanished. And so I agreed to stay on and become a colleague of Dr. Paul Teirstein, the man who was my mentor.

During my early years at Scripps, I devoted all my time to opening coronary arteries. Wearing a lead apron, standing in a windowless cath lab, I performed over seven hundred angioplasty and stent procedures that first year.

It was appealing work—routinized, repetitive, rapid, resoundingly successful. The ability to quickly open a blood vessel, especially in an emergency setting, without the risk and invasiveness of bypass surgery, was intoxicating to me. I watched ill patients, some of whom had difficulty walking across the room, lie down on the table, submit to our ministrations, and leave the hospital free of chest pain. No blood, barely an incision or downtime. Patients wrung my hand as if I were a miracle worker. I felt heroic, but I had to keep moving. There was always another supine patient, waiting in the wings. I was exhausted by the end of the day.

There were two settings in which a patient like Paul arrived in the cardiac catheterization lab.

The first was elective: when a patient failed a stress test and was sent for a catheterization—also known as a coronary angiogram. During this test, a catheter is inserted into a large artery in the groin and threaded up to the opening of the coronary arteries. Dye or contrast is injected into the coronary artery while an X-ray camera takes pictures. Watching a TV-like monitor, I could view the heart in action. If blockages were discovered, a stent could be inserted right then and there.

The other setting was when a patient showed up in the cath lab in the middle of a heart attack, directly from the emergency room. During a heart attack, a blood vessel is abruptly closed off because of the development of a blood clot. This arterial blockage prevents blood from reaching the heart muscle, which swiftly begins to die.

At that point, time equals tissue; the more time you waste, the more damage. If a patient can be transported quickly to the cath lab, the blockage can be located and an angioplasty or a stent procedure performed.

During angioplasty, a balloon is inflated within the blocked artery to open the vessel. During a stent procedure, a metal sleeve is inserted to scaffold the artery open.

This latter scenario is how I encountered most of my patients. They didn't walk into my office on their own volition but were ushered in, ashen and terrified, having had a sobering glimpse of their own mortality.

Two hundred fifty thousand people succumb each year to sudden death—people who don't even realize they have a heart problem.[1]

Paul could have easily been one of them.

In his late forties he was the CEO of an alternative health care company, a classic workaholic who spent his life running on adrenaline.

Burly and bearded, he was a West Coast countercultural success who'd managed to bridge both worlds, as comfortable in Birkenstocks as in business suits. His steely hair was tied back in a ponytail, and his face was washed with a ruddy color that made him appear as healthy as he believed he was.

The weight of Paul's company rested squarely on his shoulders. He was in charge of everything from profit margins to product placement. He was aware of currency fluctuations in Hong Kong and stock-market changes on Wall Street. There was no downtime factored into his life. He was always available for faxes, pages, multiple cell-phone calls. He was the type of guy who talked on his phone, perused the *The New York Times*, and kept an eye on CNN while jogging on a treadmill. Except Paul had omitted the treadmill. Given his background, he was well aware of the importance of exercise and stress reduction, but he hadn't quite found a slot for it in his busy schedule.

Having recently hiked to ten thousand feet and fathered a baby daughter, he felt not only at the apex of his life but invincible as well.

He reminded me of the guy who said, "I thought death might make an exception with me."

The year I met him, Paul's company had fallen into financial trouble. On the day of his heart attack, he'd been called in front of a shareholders' meeting to defend the company's business decisions and losses.

It was a tense gathering. As the company representative, he found himself the recipient of angry questions. But Paul savoured performing under pressure.

However, on this occasion, the confrontation felt different. Standing at the podium, he noticed a pressure in the middle of his chest along with a massive wave of nausea. He loosened his tie and tried to ignore it, continuing his talk.

"As you can see, the dip in our valuation is a direct result of the nationwide equity slump," he said, holding on to the podium and referring to his PowerPoint presentation.

As the questioning continued, he also began to sweat profusely and noted a discomfort in his left arm. Although Paul knew these classic signs of a heart attack, he didn't even consider the possibility. He'd never had a heart problem, and he considered himself quite fit.

In truth, Paul was harbouring blockages in three major arteries. Fatty deposits, called plaque, had been forming for years, caused by a combination of factors—a rich diet, genetics, inactivity, and chronic stress. As these deposits had continued to build up, they had narrowed his arteries and reduced blood flow to his heart.

Most heart attacks occur when a blockage is less than 50 percent. At this percentage, you may have no symptoms and even pass an exercise stress test, which may only pick up blockages greater than 70 percent. It is not uncommon to hear that someone had a stress test one week and died of a heart attack the next. It isn't until there is a blockage of 70 percent or more that a person displays the kind of symptoms Paul had begun to develop—chest tightness, sweating, and shortness of breath.

His condition didn't reach critical mass until he was confronted at the stockholders' meeting. It was then that a cascade of events came together in a potentially lethal way. Under pressure, Paul began to produce stress hormones, which caused his blood pressure and heart rate to increase and caused his arteries to grow even narrower. Adrenaline, the major stress hormone, is even known to make platelets stickier and raise cholesterol.

A blockage or plaque is like a pimple in the arterial wall. As Paul grew increasingly stressed, the cap on one of these pimples ruptured, the blood became exposed to the sticky material in the plaque, platelets began to stick, and a clot formed that closed off one of his arteries.

It wasn't until he became light-headed and developed shortness of breath that he understood that he was in serious trouble.

"I'm going to collapse," he blurted out as he staggered offstage. Unbuttoning his collar, he went into an anteroom and lay down on the floor.

When one of his colleagues found him there, he called 911.

Minutes later, Paul was strapped onto a gurney and carried off. He was no longer Paul Ross, health care maverick, wealthy investor, self-confident entrepreneur. His identity had been swiftly pared down to the essentials the EMTs were calling out: "White male, MI, BP 190 over 100, pulse 130." His stock port-folio and profit-and-loss statements meant nothing in the lit interior of the ambulance, where an oxygen mask was strapped over his face. Paul found himself searching the faces of the attendants, trying to decipher what they were thinking. From their grim looks, it didn't look good.

It was when he reached the emergency room that Paul received the most frightening signal. After scanning the results of his tests, the attending physician muttered grimly, "It's the widowmaker," referring to a particular blockage in one of the main blood vessels—the left anterior descending. At the sound of this term, Paul flashed on an image of his wife clutching their young daughter, standing in the doorway of their home, bereft and alone.

An emergency angioplasty was performed on Paul: A catheter with a small balloon at the tip was threaded into his blocked artery and inflated to stretch it and flatten the plaque. In forty-eight hours, he was released from the hospital, and that was when the real heavy lifting began.

He arrived in my office a week later, still pale and shaken, flanked by his slender wife and infant daughter, with tawny curls and Paul's gray eyes.

Encountering a new physician, especially after a heart attack, can feel like meeting with God. This stranger holds not only your data but its interpretation, the key to your future treatment. No wonder that Paul, like many of my patients, arrived at our appointment so flustered and tongue-tied that he barely asked a question.

But I consider working with a heart patient a collaboration in which neither of us can succeed alone. Solving cardiac problems requires more than technical skills. In order for lasting change to occur, it's not enough for me to enter the scene like a mechanic, to unblock an artery or treat a leaking valve; a patient has to be fully involved in his or her own healing.

Even though I'm the specialist who has studied complex manuals and seen hundreds of different cases, patients know their bodies like no one else; in this sense, *they're* the definitive experts.

Because most of my patients are unable to fathom the reality of their hearts, I always include concrete visuals on a first visit, drawing a diagram that illustrates each particular problem. In Paul's case, after diagramming his arteries, I shaded in the location of his three blockages.

"I still can't believe this," he said, staring down at the drawing.

Paul had many of the key risk factors that I call the "sixpack." His lipids were terrible; he carried his weight in the midline. He had high blood pressure and low HDL or "good" cholesterol. He was underexercised. The only things he didn't have against him were diabetes and cigarette smoking.

However, his blood tests revealed that he had metabolic syndrome, which predisposed him to diabetes mellitus. Three out of four of the following indicators indicate the existence of this syndrome: an enlarged abdominal girth for men (greater than forty inches), high blood pressure, low HDL, and high triglycerides. Paul had all four.

I drew another picture of an artery and explained to Paul that some bad cholesterol (LDL) is small in size. These small particles are more prone to get into the vessel wall and build up plaque. Small particles keep company with high triglycerides and low HDL and account for 50 percent of all vascular disease in men. The diet supplement and medication regimen that I was going to prescribe for Paul would address these issues.

This narration was taking too long, I could tell. Paul was becoming increasingly impatient.

"All right," he said. "Let's hear it."

"First, we'll tackle your diet. Triglycerides come from simple carbohydrates and sugar."

"I don't eat any of that," he insisted.

I began to read off the list of common high-glycemic-index foods: "This means honey, bagels, pretzels, white rice, crackers, white bread, potatoes, alcohol, cookies, cake, candy, popcorn . . ." and I saw he hadn't realized how many foods this list included.

"From now on, I want you to eat only low-glycemic-index foods that won't increase your insulin level, create weight around the midline, and release inflammatory factors. Make sure you have plenty of green vegetables and omega-3 fatty acids, such as in wild salmon and trout."

Instead of having Paul drink fruit juices, I steered him toward water and herbal teas. Instead of tropical fruits such as pineapple, papaya, and mango, I recommended that he eat low-sugar fruits such as apples, berries, peaches, pears, and plums.

Finally, I showed him the results of the Lyon Heart Study, one of the best nutritional studies in cardiology. It was a four year follow-up of more than six hundred men and women in France who had experienced a first heart attack, which put them at high risk for a second one. Nearly half the participants were advised to eat a Mediterranean-style diet rich in fruits, vegetables, fish, olive oil, and beans. I could tell that he was clearly impressed with the data, which showed a marked decrease in cardiovascular events, cancer, and death in those participants randomized to this Mediterranean-style diet.[2]

But one of Paul's most troublesome risk factors remained his stress, which now encompassed not only his work but his heart disease.

As I wrote down these factors on the left side of the page and our goals on the right, he jiggled his leg and fumbled with a cell phone, his dismay and anxiety apparent.

"How could this have happened? I am not even fifty! I already take fish oil, coenzyme Q10, and every antioxidant in the book."

"You're a work junkie, Paul," his wife said softly. "I don't think supplements can fix all your problems."

"What are you talking about?"

"You never stop. You're like an engine in overdrive. You don't even sit down to eat anymore."

Yet even as she spoke, Paul began fussing again with his cell phone. "Damn, I've got to get this."

He stood and paced the office, talking loudly. "Chuck, I told you to sell if the price dropped below thirty. . . . I don't care! Check the Dow, it just opened. . . ."

Whenever I see a new patient, I'm always aware that it isn't a disease sitting across from me but a person, trailing a complex history behind him or her. Paul's mask had slipped and given me a glimpse of what lurked under his sweet-faced demeanor. His fidgety legs, his red face, and his anxious manner allowed me to peek at who he really was.

His wife and I remained silent until he finished his call. Then, as he turned back to us, he seemed to realize that he'd just provided us with a tableau of what had brought him—and his heart—to this juncture.

"Paul, you've got some serious decisions to make," I told him when he sat down again. "You're on the tracks, and the train's coming. You can stand there or you can get off. It's your choice."

Paul tossed his cell phone on the table and looked at his daughter, who, as if on cue, opened her mouth and began to cry.

"She's getting a tooth. God, I hadn't even noticed. . . ." Paul said. Then his own face collapsed and he sat for a moment, his head bowed.

"I want off the tracks," he finally murmured. "Help me get off. Please."

Some people who grapple with enormous amounts of stress actually flourish. Athletes, actors, currency traders, all talk about thriving on the adrenaline rush. These people are called hardy or resilient by psychologists, since they are able to thrive under pressure and high demand.

They're able to take advantage of a spike in stress hormones during the day for performance and allow these levels to drop back to normal at night.

But most of us register stress much more deeply, receiving a good dose as soon as we awake. An alarm startles us from sleep, beginning a flow of stress hormones that continues throughout the day. Honking horns, looming deadlines, ringing phones, all shift our heart into high gear. As blood pounds into the heart with extra force, it's as if our body is screaming inside us: "Fire!" Chronic activation of this stress response is damaging to our cardiovascular system, causing high blood pressure, in-flammation, and blood vessel damage. For most of us, the only time we get a break from this constant bath of stress is when—and if—we sleep at night.

So how could a susceptible person like Paul minimize his risk of stress without hiding away in a closet or encasing himself in a plastic bubble?

One way was to identify and then avoid personal triggers —those situations that literally sent him through the roof, ratcheted up his blood pressure, and started his stress hormones flowing. He admitted that even simple things such as getting stuck in a bank line or being put on a voice loop on the phone could increase his heart rate.

Another way was for Paul to learn techniques that allowed him to gain control over anxious sensations whenever he felt them starting to occur.

Research has shown that stress reducers such as visualization, hypnosis, deep breathing, meditation, and yoga have measurable effects on cardiac risk, helping to relax arteries and reduce levels of stress hormones.[3]

But even this wasn't enough for Paul. What do you do if your whole life is stressful?

When I first met Paul, I recognized a cluster of behaviors and beliefs that were all faintly familiar, like a melody I couldn't quite identify. Overbooked, overworked, and full of denial. Smart, strong-willed, yet almost blind to certain aspects of his own life. Who exactly did he remind me of?

All week I thought about it. Then one night I looked up at my exhausted face in the steamy bathroom mirror, and I blushed at my own thick headedness.

Of course, it was myself. In my thirties, I was a classic type A overachiever, stressed out, underexercised, with my own complicated heart.

For years I'd led a typical doctor's lifestyle, working long hours, feeding off the cookies and pizza families left at the nurses' station, my prime exercise walking across the parking lot to my car.

The blinkered single-mindedness that had gotten me out of Bensonhurst and through medical school had begun to show on me. My own cholesterol level was higher than some of my illest patients—over three hundred at one count. Heart disease ran like a river on both sides of my family, and whether I acknowledged it or not, those waters formed a tributary in me.

On the other hand, I knew that I wasn't simply my genes. I'd spent my life proving how different I was from the girls I'd grown up around. I was independent, free, and educated, beholden to no one.

I was the expert, the doctor, the successful young woman. I had all the knowledge and answers; I knew the latest techniques. Nothing could possibly be wrong with my heart. Right?

But then there was my stress.

I was perpetually on call, juggling patients, obligations, meetings. Often a patient was waiting for me in my office while I was in the middle of a catheterization on someone else. The sense of being pulled by multiple strands of obligation created a sense of rushing breathlessness, as if I were running out of oxygen.

When I caught a reflection of myself in the hospital windows, stethoscope bobbing, I looked like some hunted creature from a scary movie, a streak of silver and white.

I knew all the research—that stress was comparable to hypertension as a risk factor for heart disease;[4] that the

American Institute of Stress reported that 75 percent to 90 percent of all visits to health care practitioners were due to stress-related disorders;[5] that the Mayo Clinic had concluded that psychological stress was the strongest indicator of future cardiac events.[6]

I'd read studies linking stress and cholesterol that dated back to the 1950s. One of these studies demonstrated that when fifty-five men were subjected to stress by cold-water immersion, an immediate rise in their cholesterol occurred.[7] Job stresses with associated time pressure, repetitive assembly-line work, overwork, and increased responsibility were shown to raise serum cholesterol. Accountants showed continuous monthly rises in cholesterol, despite maintaining a consistent diet, which peaked at the end of the fiscal year.[8]

I knew this data better than anyone, regularly ticking off these studies and statistics to my patients. Even so, a shell of separateness had gradually been hardening around me—one that kept me feeling apart from, even above, my patients and at the same time creating the illusion that I, the person with all the answers, was impervious to illness myself.

Then, as I continued my work at Scripps, I began to have a series of unfolding realizations. One was an awareness that my medical practice was making me less a doctor than a high-tech plumber, trained to sit and wait for someone to have a heart attack rather than to prevent one from happening.

When I'd first arrived, I'd been so excited about my work that I didn't question why a guy who'd had bypass surgery was back to see me with reclogged arteries just five years later. I simply stented him and moved on. But as time passed, I began to feel that someone had installed a revolving door in the cardiac catheterization lab when I wasn't looking, one that kept ushering the same patients back onto my table.

My schedule resembled an alumni gathering; I liked my patients, but I was getting together with them on a far too regular basis. I not only recognized the names on my weekly schedule but could predict their blockages before we did the angiograms.

The admitting clerk shrugged when I seemed alarmed about this, as if to say, "Be grateful. We are busy." And it was true: This was our business, treating sick people. Who was going to pay us if everyone was well?

But it also became clear that stenting arteries was creating a whole new problem. When we expanded an artery with balloons and stents, in some patients the artery reacted as if it had been injured and began to repair itself in response.

We found ourselves with a new problem called restenosis, the formation of scar tissue inside the artery—an event that occurred approximately 20 percent of the time, sometimes repeatedly. We discovered that one way to halt this process was by placing gamma radiation, iridium 192, inside the artery.[9] This was a major advance in interventional cardiology, pioneered by Dr.

Paul Teirstein. With intracoronary radiation, approximately 70 percent of those who formed scar tissue never formed it again. Today we have new stents, coated with antibiotics and chemotherapeutic agents and capable of blocking scar tissue from forming approximately 90 percent of the time. Still, I felt that something profound was being hinted at that we still weren't apprehending. Suppressing natural healing, while beneficial for stent success, seemed like progress in the wrong direction. We were blocking the heart's healing power instead of learning how to harness it.

And despite all our interventions, despite over a million stents in 2002, five hundred thousand open-heart or bypass surgeries, cardiovascular disease still was America's biggest killer. The public was spending billions of dollars on cutting and pasting, yet after we mopped up the mess and sent our patients down to intensive care, I'd find them sitting up in their beds happily eating roast-beef sandwiches slathered with mayo. Before they'd even exited the hospital grounds, they were already in the process of reclosing the arteries I had just opened.

The attitude of some doctors and nurses was, "They're sick, let them eat what they want."

But by serving this to patients in a hospital setting, we were in effect saying, "This is okay for you."

My patients were also starting to come to me with questions I couldn't answer and treatments I couldn't validate.

When my forty-five-year-old patient Paula, who had angina, asked me how she could sleep without taking sleeping pills or how she could manage stress without taking sedatives, my mind went blank.

When dapper old Mr. Federico, of the Brylcreemed pompadour, confessed that his blood pressure medicine had made him impotent and what was he going to do if he couldn't have sex, I was even more embarrassed than his blushing wife sitting beside him, because I didn't know what to tell him.

During an office visit when I asked my patient Mae what vitamins and supplements she was taking, she plopped a shopping bag at my feet.

"What's this?"

"My herbs."

I peeked in at bottle after bottle of potions and tinctures—cat's claw, black cohosh, dandelion root, milk thistle—half of them sounding as if they'd been gathered from the side of the road.

"How do you know about this stuff or how much to take?"

She shrugged. "Friends tell me. I look it up on the Web."

"Wouldn't you rather try a statin instead?"

"I don't want to take drugs—too many side effects."

What did it mean that this woman, educated and savvy, was willing to take these supplements rather than a drug that I was advising with all my years of medical experience?

Another afternoon, I had stopped at a light in down-town San Diego when I saw a patient of mine, Roger, emerging from a storefront, straightening his shirt as he walked.

I looked up at the sign, but it was written in Chinese. My first thought was that he'd just visited a massage parlor. As the light changed, he caught sight of me and waved jauntily as I sped past.

At our next appointment, I was studying his test results when he said: "I saw you last week when I was coming out of my treatment."

"Treatment?"

"Yeah, I've been going to Dr. Yee for acupuncture, and I really think it's helping; he was a medical doctor in Beijing before he moved here. He does energy work."

Sure, I thought, turning away. *Anyone can say they were a doctor in Beijing—how would you ever check?*

"And how exactly does this help you?"

Roger smiled. "Well, he spent a long time talking to me about the way stress was showing up in my upper body. He's working to balance my chi—something about meridians."

Standing in my sparkling clean office, I imagined a basement cubbyhole with unsterilized needles. I had the typical Westerner's blend of cynicism and condescension about these treatments, of which I was vastly ignorant.

Like a jilted girlfriend, I was getting the distinct impression that my patients were wandering away from me for the company of more alluring and attentive alternative therapists who had more time and better tools than I.

It wasn't so much that I disapproved of these treatments as that I had so little knowledge of them. I didn't want my patients hiding shopping bags of herbs from me. I wanted to figure out what was wrong with the care for which I had spent my whole life training.

When I looked at the data, I was shocked to find that according to a 2002 government survey, *nearly half* of all Americans used mind-body interventions, ranging from deep breathing and progressive muscle relaxation to hypnosis, guided imagery, and meditation.[10]

I found data showing the burgeoning number of visits to alternative medicine practitioners as opposed to primary care doctors; billions of dollars paid out of pocket by patients to practitioners who by and large had no degree from a medical school.

I saw the reasons for this at work each day. Our hospital halls were teeming with patients wandering from one impersonal scope and scan to the next, repeating the litany of their personal histories. In the busyness of an acute care setting, it was difficult to find much sympathizing, synthesizing, or empathizing.

Yet I knew that traditional medicine was good at many things. We excelled at acute care and trauma. If you have a heart attack, you need an emergency room in a conventional medical facility.

As I was pondering this data, another event caught my attention. I'd inserted a stent into a fifty-four-year-old man who'd had a recent heart attack—a typical procedure I'd done a thousand times before.

After he returned home the next day, he called my office, frantic.

"Last week, I thought I was healthy," he told my secretary. "Now I'm on six medications, and there's this metal sleeve in my artery. I'm completely traumatized. Do you have some kind of support group? I need to talk to someone."

When my secretary told me this, I dismissed the whole notion; I did ten stents a day; what was the big deal?

"There's no such thing as a stent support group here," I said, filling out a form and signing a release in my usual multitasking way.

But later that day, as I stood at my local car dealership, I watched a technician bent over the hood of a patron's car, explaining his transmission problem and the various options he could try. And it dawned on me that he was spending more time with this guy's *car* than I had spent with my stent patient's heart.

After that, I couldn't stop thinking about his call for help. I'd never considered the implications of having a "piece of metal in the heart." A stent might be an everyday occurrence for me, but it had changed this man's life.

They say that when you're ready, the teacher appears. It was at this point of transition that I was approached by Dean Ornish and asked if I'd take part in his research.

Ornish was one of the first physicians to demonstrate that coronary disease could be reversed without surgery using diet, exercise, yoga, meditation, and group support.[11]

I still found it difficult to accept that my heart patients would really benefit from these interventions instead of hardware and medication. But I recognized that there was a paradigm shift going on and it wasn't coming from the American College of Cardiology but from the patient. I agreed that we would be part of the Multicenter Lifestyle Heart Trial.

When we started the project, we needed a nurse, and Rauni King came in for an interview. A certified holistic nurse with twenty years' experience in intensive care, she was involved in energy healing, based on Eastern models.

During the interview, she described her experience using healing touch with ICU patients, but I felt my attention drifting as she talked about auras and chakras. I was now experiencing a growing split, half of me firmly rooted in the old scientific world where I had trained and suffered and been rewarded—and the other half tilted toward this alternative world that my patients apparently found so satisfying. It was hard to let loose of my skeptical side, the hectoring voice that felt like screaming out, "Meridians! Energy tracts! *What are you talking about?*"

Had I spent a decade of my life in teaching hospitals. in order to entertain this kind of esoteric stuff? Rauni was serene and self-assured, and we hired her, but I couldn't say I was totally convinced.

Then I caught a viral infection from a patient, and it changed everything.

Of course, sickness was an everyday occurrence in my environment, except it wasn't one that happened *to me*. A naturally hardy person, I was proud of my constitution and ability to ward off viruses and bugs. But suddenly I was transformed into this pale, weak, and listless body draped over the bed. My lymph nodes were swollen, and I had so many sores in my mouth and throat that I couldn't eat.

Like Paul, it wasn't until I was literally knocked off my feet that I was able to see what I couldn't discern when I was up on my physician's pedestal—that being ill challenged your whole sense of self. It was a chastening reminder that anyone could become a patient at any moment.

After a week of being unable to move, I pulled myself up to attend an important meeting and ran into Rauni, who took one look at me and said, "You really look sick."

"I am; I can't seem to shake it."

"Let's go into one of the treatment rooms. I want to check your energy field."

"I don't think I have one," I said, but I staggered after her anyway.

I'd been brought down so low that my resistance and skepticism were gone. Just like my patients, I wanted to feel better, and I didn't particularly care what the treatment was called.

In the room, Rauni had me lie down and began "scanning my field," as she called it.

Later I would discover that the practice of healing touch is based on the notion that the body, mind, and emotions form a complex energy field that can be accessed. Practitioners believe that in a healthy person, the energy field is patterned and ordered—and that illness occurs when the energy field is disrupted.

"Your energy's completely unbalanced," Rauni murmured after hovering over me a few minutes. "I'm going to start clearing your field."

"Okay."

I waited for her to touch me, but she never did. In fact, she held her hands several inches above my head, moving slowly toward my feet.

I closed my eyes to keep from being critical, and then I stopped thinking at all. Time disappeared; I fell off a cliff into a kind of oblivion.

What I felt was hard to explain—a sense of soothing, as if a strong light were being beamed all over me.

I wasn't a person who could lie still for five minutes, let alone an hour. Yet I found myself transfixed by a loop of warmth, a kind of voltage that seemed to travel through me.

I forgot about opening my eyes. I forgot about my body. I just *was*.

When Rauni finally said, "Okay, I'm finished," I opened my eyes and felt as if my life force had been restored. My head was clear, and I felt stable when I got to my feet.

After a week of profound weakness, I thought I might actually be able to return to work.

"What did you *do*?"

"I cleared your energy field," Rauni said matter-of-factly.

But more than my energy had been unblocked. My mind had been opened as well.

After my experience with Rauni, I decided that I shouldn't ask my patients to try anything that I wasn't willing to do myself. I shelved any misgivings and undertook the Ornish program, right alongside them. Still holding on to my belief in evidence-based research, I became my own experiment and turned my critical, scientific eye on myself.

I sat in support groups, not as a leader but as a participant, listening to how terrifying it was to be told your heart was ailing, hearing how intimidating and superior doctors could be. After a lifetime of pepperoni pizza, I made an about-face and became vegetarian. I sat in yoga, struggling to empty my mind for even a second of the clutter of worries that I realized were always there: *Where had I put Mrs. Jackson's electrolyte studies? How many stents did I have scheduled the next morning? Had I paid the mortgage?*

I mimicked the woman beside me, a survivor of two heart attacks, who was humming "Ommmmm" while meditating, her face serene. I completed the final topple from my pedestal. These patients were the ones teaching *me*.

And as I watched patients learn how to manage their stress, I began to do it myself. I told my secretary: "One thing at a time from now on; don't overbook me. I'm taking a break for lunch starting this week, and during that time, I don't want to be disturbed."

My secretary looked at me as if I'd lost my mind. Having a nervous breakdown or a heart attack of my own would have been less shocking than this attempt at prevention.

I began making it my business to emerge each day from the windowless cath lab to stand, like a groundhog, inhaling the brilliant salt and spume of ocean air. I took a full breath from deep in my abdomen as they taught me to do in yoga, not the little hyperventilating breaths that left me panting like my dog.

It was liberating to make these changes. I felt them in the core of my body, as if a heavy cape had been lifted from my shoulders and flung aside. I still had a stressful job, but I was able to avoid situations that expressly rang my bell and drove me up the wall. No one else could do this for me; I had to do it for myself.

And slowly, surely, right alongside my patients, I began seeing results. I found myself feeling stronger, sleeping better. Eventually my cholesterol numbers lowered, without medication, from 320 to 99.

Rauni and I were both so won over by the dramatic success of the program not only in our patients' lives but in our own that we began to wonder if there were a way of bringing these two worlds together—not choosing one or the other, but combining the best of both. This ultimately resulted in the formation of the Scripps Center for Integrative Medicine, which weaves the best of modern high technology, nutrition, and exercise with evidence-based alternative therapies such as acupuncture, healing touch, meditation, and yoga.

All of which is a long way of saying something very elemental and simple: When I sat in front of Paul and suggested that he needed to make some drastic changes if he wanted to live, I felt certain of what I was saying because I was living, breathing proof.

Luckily, for many of Paul's specific problems, there were fairly straightforward answers. To change his sedentary lifestyle, he hired a personal trainer. To lose weight, he radically altered his diet.

But there's no way I could ever have written a prescription for the profound advice he eventually decided to follow: "There's no place that isn't watching; you have to change your life."[12] For the final piece of the puzzle—his extraordinarily stressful lifestyle—Paul decided to step away from the daily operations of his business and became a consultant, letting his partners deal with the hassles and daily grind. He moved himself out of the hot seat, so that he was no longer the prime recipient of responsibility. He let go of the reins and stepped back.

For someone like Paul, whose identity was tied to being a dominant force in the workplace and the main breadwinner at home, this was a monumental step.

Ultimately, he and his family left California and moved to a farm back east, where he rekindled an old passion, playing the cello, and concentrated on appreciating the family he'd had so little time to relish in the past.

For patients like Paul, who are literally stopped in their tracks by this medical emergency, heart attacks are often wakeup calls. The drastic upheaval of illness throws into stark relief how cut off from meaning their lives have become.

As he lay on the gurney heading into the emergency room, Paul had watched the blur of stricken faces looking down at him and found that he was thinking not of profit margins or stock prices but of a scene from *Our Town*, a play he'd seen in high school some thirty years before.

In the play, Emily, a young woman who died in childbirth, decides to leave the world of the dead and return to her previous life. But when she steps back into the morning of her twelfth birthday, she's overcome by the youth and beauty of her parents. And she's struck by how much of everyday life, with its triumphs and sorrows, she once took for granted.

In the end, she feels so agonized by the transience and preciousness of human existence that she asks to return to the graveyard.

"They don't understand," she says of the living as the stars come out in the cemetery sky.[13]

Paul now claims that the day of his heart attack was the best day of his life. As the months passed, he realized that, unlike Emily and all the real lives behind the grim statistics, he was receiving a gift he could never barter or pay for—a chance to rise out of the haze of unconscious living, hang up the phone, log off the computer, make music again, and open his arms to embrace his ordinary, precious life.

Paul and I have this gift in common. Because the other person I think of when I'm asked whether stress can cause a heart attack was that harried version of myself, the hunted creature I used to glimpse in hospital windows, trying to outpace the fate of her own complex heart.

Chapter Four

Echoes of Anger

The heart is not simply suspended in a body but in a culture, a place, a time. We are all aware of the traditional risk factors for coronary disease that are physically related—obesity, high cholesterol, hypertension, smoking, diabetes, a sedentary lifestyle. But these factors may fail to identify 50 percent of patients with coronary disease. We now know that diseases of the heart can also be caused by other, more subtle factors such as isolation, depression, and hostility that have to do with not only how we live but how we experience our lives.

There are recent studies suggesting that hostility, in particular, may be more predictive of coronary disease than more traditional factors such as smoking and high cholesterol. Researchers have found that heart attacks, angina, or other symptoms of coronary disease occurred much more often among men who measured as hostile on a personality test than in those who had more conventional risk factors. Indeed, the only such measurement that predicted heart disease risk more accurately than hostility was low levels of HDL, or "good" cholesterol.[1]

In 1959, Drs. Meyer Friedman and Ray Rosenman famously reported that individuals who exhibited type A behavior—the same rushed, competitive, deadline-driven type of personality I happen to have—displayed a higher risk for having a heart attack.[2] Later studies have found that it is not this personality type per se but rather certain elements of it, such as cynicism and hostility, that are risk factors most associated with increased cardiovascular risk. We understand intuitively that overt hostility is dangerous. When a driver full of road rage suddenly appears in our rearview window, we gladly let him pass, distancing ourselves from his anger.

But why exactly is hostility so toxic to the heart?

Feelings of hostility—along with mild to moderate depression—in healthy men have also been shown to raise levels of a protein, IL-6, a maker of inflammation that may be involved in the process that causes arterial thickening.[3]

People with high hostility levels have more pronounced heart-rate responses and blood pressures when placed in anger provoking situations. They also are more likely to engage in risky behaviors, such as smoking, overeating, and not exercising.[4]

Stress hormones such as cortisol and epinephrine are maximized in situations where people feel anger and little control over their life circumstances, resulting in higher cholesterol and blood sugar levels.

There is also evidence that people who are furious at the world are more likely to develop atrial fibrillation, a possibly dangerous heartbeat abnormality.[5]

From the body's point of view, a hostile or angry thought registers as a ringing bell, warning the body to ready itself for a fight. To prepare for action, the heartbeat quickens; muscles tense; stress hormones are released; vision and hearing become more acute and focused; the whole body contracts. These reactions typically fade once a person no longer feels threatened. But an angry person may carry these reactions within him as his daily state, a cauldron of chronic rage.

Suppressed emotions, or ones we are unconscious of, don't just simmer on the back burner indefinitely; they eventually manifest themselves on a physical level and are reflected in our bodies as physical symptoms. And if you lift up the veil of hostility and anger, in my experience, you usually find some kind of emotional pain.

Just like the heart, the relationship between a patient and a doctor exists within a cultural context. And in our culture at the present moment, the model is too much technology and not enough time. Therapeutic relationships with empathic family physicians have often been replaced with rushed, impersonal encounters with technicians and machines. One of my patients came to see me after having a physical so swift and cursory that the physician didn't even listen to his heart. Another told me how her father had been told by his physician that he had prostate cancer while the doctor was turned the other way, rushing to fill out an insurance form.

"Could you take a moment and look at my father when you tell him he has cancer," she said to the doctor.

In spite of studies that have long reported that doctors who attend to what their patients tell them have improved clinical outcomes, the constant complaint in patient satisfaction surveys is, "My doctor doesn't listen to me!" One often cited study reports that doctors, on average, interrupt patients only eighteen seconds after they begin to talk.[6]

The pressure on physicians to see increased numbers of patients has resulted in the brief time a patient and physician have together being dominated by technical areas and physical symptoms, depriving patients of the opportunity to recount their full story, which may have important and complex emotional content.

If a physician is allocated 17.9 minutes (the average length of a managed care office visit)[7] with a patient and the clock is ticking, she's not going to dawdle to ask searching questions or take the time to delve into the deeper reasons a patient may have come to see her—which may not be divulged initially. The system encourages her to listen until a diagnostic knowledge tree springs into her mind, saying, "A leaky valve! An aortic aneurysm," then to lapse into automatic, ordering tests and procedures based on this rapid recognition.

Patients aren't alone in finding the quality of medical treatment disturbing. "If I'm not fast, I'm fired," a doctor friend told me after receiving complaints about the short amount of time she was allotted for patients' yearly physicals.

Physicians also have much to gain in terms of satisfaction through better communication. According to Mack Lipkin, founding president of the American

Academy on Physician and Patient, "There's an epidemic of burnout," with a high turnover of doctors in health plans. "The most significant factor in physician satisfaction is the patient encounter. Physicians with better skills have better quality patient encounters and are more satisfied and less likely to burn out."[8]

The inability—or unwillingness—of doctors to fully communicate with patients has far-reaching implications—from an inability to gather information, to the ordering of wasteful tests, to a failure to engage patients in their own healing.

I know the statistics well—the eighteen-second interruption, the 17.9-minute visit—they were statistics I struggled daily to keep out of my own practice and life.

A confluence of these issues converged in my patient Russ, a forty-six-year-old man with severe coronary artery disease who came to see me one summer morning.

A handsome almond-skinned man, he entered my office at Scripps haltingly, his head hung low, flanked by his wife and adolescent son, who hovered anxiously around him like satellites.

With his flowing white hair and solemn face, he looked like a wounded prince in a funeral frieze. His face was particularly striking, both noble and devastated. I thought I detected a hint of Native American blood in his high cheekbones, but he hadn't noted any nationality on his paperwork.

The family entered the office on a still breeze of dread. This wasn't surprising. I'm often the doctor of last resort, the one patients are sent to when there's little hope—or when their physicians have given up.

But I don't believe in death sentences; I've seen too many people who've lived when their doctors have written them off, and too many others who've died without clear medical causes.

Once they sat down, Russ said, "I just want you to know that I'm only here because my wife forced me."

"Okay," I said tentatively, thinking, *What an opening!*

But this was better than his second line: "My life's finished," he went on. "The doctors say I should put my affairs in order."

Russ's terse tone and tight face told me how diminished he'd been by his heart disease and his doctors' bleak prognosis. His spirit seemed shattered, and he radiated a deep distress.

It was clear that he was presenting me with his body, but only reluctantly and under duress, because he considered it already defeated. *Dead Man Walking.* This was the image that swept through me.

On paper, Russ's cardiac situation wasn't optimistic. At forty-six, he had severe coronary artery disease and had already been denied a heart transplant. Although he'd undergone a coronary bypass a year earlier, many of the grafts had already begun to fail. His triglyceride and cholesterol levels were high, and he continued to suffer from angina, mainly connected with stress.

However, people don't live on paper. A heart can't possibly be fathomed simply through catheterization readings or cholesterol levels. These may have been Russ's external data, the test results that could be stuffed in the manila folder on my desk, but as I have learned over the years, the deep stories carved into the hearts of patients can be told only by them.

As the interview progressed, it was clear that Russ planned to keep himself under wraps. Whenever I prompted him to talk, he averted his stony face and let his wife speak instead.

A tiny woman with a worried face, she showed no reluctance about recounting all of her husband's limitations. "We've been broke ever since his bypass," she told me, twisting a Kleenex. "It's impossible to make it on disability. Russ can't even install our air conditioner anymore."

I'd already noticed Russ's fists, clenched in his lap, and as his wife continued her complaints, I saw them clench even tighter. This guy was as rigid as steel.

I knew it was going to be challenging to break through to Russ, but I tried all my usual methods: I told him about cases similar to his that I'd successfully treated; I asked him searching questions; I engaged his family. But as we continued talking, I still hadn't gotten a handle on him, and I'd elicited only the most meager collection of personal facts beyond what were already in my file: that he had once been a day laborer who installed heaters and air conditioners, that he had a black belt in karate, and that his heart disease had left him housebound, unemployed, and struggling to survive on disability.

His identity had been based on being physically strong and capable. He could no longer work, walk, or exercise without experiencing angina, a temporary decrease of oxygen to the heart muscle signalling that the muscle isn't receiving enough blood.

I tell my patients that angina is their heart speaking to them, saying, "Pay attention!"

Every person experiences angina in a different fashion. One person may notice chest tightness when he's walking up a hill. Another a tightness in her back as she makes a bed or a jaw ache when jogging.

Russ's angina was trying to tell him something, but deciphering the message of the heart can be as difficult as understanding a foreign language. I felt Russ's heart was crying out in some sharp, specific way, but what was it saying?

As a cardiologist, I find that my hardest task isn't performing an angioplasty or inserting a stent into a blocked artery. In fact, these procedures are a breeze compared with the job I had in front of me, trying to instill hope in this frozen mountain of a man.

I continued to search Russ's face, looking for a point of entry, but the blinds were drawn. All my questions were answered by one-word answers. He wouldn't meet my eyes. How was I ever going to get through to this guy?

After reviewing his test results, I discussed my plan to stent his arteries in order to increase blood flow to his heart.

"I've had many patients like you who have found real relief from angina after having their artery opened." I drew a diagram to illustrate how the stent would scaffold open the blockage. "Afterward, we can look at ways you can change your life to help reverse your heart disease."

Russ absorbed all this in his inscrutable way and, in the end, reluctantly agreed to the stent procedure. But I suspected this was chiefly because his wife and son had begged him, rather than because of anything I'd said. It was clear from his demeanour that he had little belief that it would help.

He didn't trust doctors, and who could blame him? They had done the unpardonable: taken his hope and snuffed it out.

On the morning of Russ's surgery, I noticed his wife and son huddled together in the waiting room over cups of coffee. The waiting room is the most terrifying spot in the hospital: family and loved ones sitting with tattered, out-of-date magazines while the fate of their loved ones is decided in the parallel universe of the operating room.

The stent procedure was one I'd done so many times over the years that it had become my specialty. And with a 99 percent success rate, I felt confident of a successful outcome for Russ.

"You're going to feel better after this," I reassured Russ as he was wheeled into the cath lab, but all I got from him was a dubious nod.

About two hours into the procedure, an extremely rare but major complication occurred. To my disbelief, Russ's vessel ruptured and a fresh lake of blood began spreading inside his chest. This was the worst possible occurrence, and one that happens in less than 1 percent.

"Oh no!" I whispered, and the surgery nurse looked up at me in alarm.

I worked to stop the bleeding, but to no avail.

"I think Dr. Morgan's on call; would you page him?" I asked the nurse after a few more minutes.

I was frantically trying everything I could think of to stop the flow when the heart surgeon rushed in and looked at Russ's chart.

"This isn't good, Mimi," he murmured. "You know he's not a candidate for bypass. What are you going to do?"

"I hoped you'd have some bright idea."

"Sorry," he said as he returned to his rounds. It was true that Russ's vessels were small and his chances of surviving emergency bypass surgery were slim. We needed to come up with another solution. While my hands kept busy, I directed my frantic mind to textbook cases I'd read about, anecdotes I'd heard, but none of them applied to the situation here.

The next time I looked up, two hours had passed and I still hadn't made any headway. How long could I keep going with this? I wondered. I was concerned about Russ, not about tiring myself. I was so flooded with adrenaline that my own heart was banging in my chest. I noticed that Russ had begun moving his legs, which was dangerous, given the site of his catheter insertion. "I'm dizzy, Doc," he murmured. "I'm having chest pain."

In the next few minutes, his blood pressure steadily dropped; he was beginning to die right in front of my eyes. I couldn't have him writhing around on the table while I desperately tried to stop his bleeding, so I finally called in the anesthesiologist and had him completely sedated.

"Hang in there, everything's going to be okay. We've got to work on you some more," I murmured to Russ as he went under, but I realized I wasn't speaking so much to him as to myself.

I imagined walking out into that waiting room and giving Russ's wife and son that awful look that conveys that a loved one has died. But the image broke apart; I couldn't visualize it. There was no way I was going to enact that scene. I had to fix this somehow.

I used every trick I'd ever heard of, but I simply couldn't seal off Russ's vessel. Approaching the fifth hour, I was woozy with fatigue when out of the blue I thought of something that I'd never used before and haven't used since: gel foam, a clotting agent that is sometimes used to block blood flow from an oozing vessel.

As I squirted the gel foam into the artery, I was amazed to see the bleeding stop.

I blinked to make sure I wasn't hallucinating.

"Did you see that?"

The nurse was as exhilarated as I was. Russ's blood pressure returned to normal, and we successfully completed the procedure.

Later, when I went into the recovery room, I walked up to Russ's gurney and stood looking down at him, lying there with closed eyes.

The anesthesia had relaxed his features, so that I could see glimpses of another face embedded in the man's—a younger, more vulnerable version of Russ.

Standing there, I flashed back to my own first hospitalization as a girl of ten—how nauseous I'd been from the anesthesia, how miserable and alone I felt, still bruised from the loss of my mother. I'd been comforted by a nurse who'd swooped in like an angel and fussed over me, tucking me in with warm blankets. She hadn't done anything particular, but the quality of her attention to me in that moment had been deeply comforting.

I was wishing that I could convey this same feeling to Russ when he opened his eyes and looked up at me, and I saw, inexplicably, that I had.

Something had passed between us in those bloody hours, something I couldn't properly quantify or explain in my surgical notes. It was a miracle that he had survived.

On our follow-up visit the next week, Russ had a different quality. He stood straighter; his eyes were brighter; he seemed infused with an *aliveness*.

I asked all the usual questions.

"How do you feel?"

"Different."

"Better?"

He seemed embarrassed to admit it.

"Yes."

He took off his shirt, and I listened to his heart. Although the small vessel that we had attempted to stent had closed, his angina was under better control. But he was still clearly weak and out of shape.

As I turned away and began filling out his chart, I heard the low murmur of his voice speaking to me.

"I'm a member of the Blackfeet tribe," he said. "My ancestors were one of the first tribes to begin moving west. We traveled in small bands—usually about twenty people—but we came together for rituals and trade. We were buffalo hunters."

I stopped in my tracks. Russ had a sonorous, melodic voice that I'd never heard in his terse replies to me in the past. In fact, I'd never heard him say so many words since we'd met. I put down my pen and turned toward him, afraid to break the spell.

"The most sacred event of our year was the sun dance, when we gathered together to fulfill vows assuring abundance of buffalo and the well-being of our tribe.

"We were able to resist intrusion by white settlers until late in the nineteenth century. It was a great devastation to us when the buffalo were driven almost to extinction. My tribe was forced to be totally dependent upon the government Indian agency in order to survive.. ."

Why is he telling me all this? the clinical part of me wondered. *What does this have to do with his heart problems?* My eye wandered to the clock; I had already run far over my allotted time with him, but I resisted the urge to interrupt.

As Russ continued speaking, my nurse stuck her head into the doorway and gave me a quizzical look. I was running way over. But I gave her a nod that meant I wanted us to be left alone. Then I did something I hadn't done since medical school. I turned off my scientist's mind, the rushed, skeptical, two-minute mind that was muttering in the background.

I put down my instruments and prescription pad, and I let my patient talk.

Our culture has its roots in a storytelling tradition.

There is something in us that yearns to tell the stories of our lives, and have them listened to in return. Research shows that in the act of deep listening and responding, a therapeutic exchange takes places, one that may help heal emotional and psychic wounds.[9]

In medicine, this kind of exchange is especially potent, since historically it is through the telling and receiving of stories that a diagnosis is found. Before angiograms and echocardiograms, this was how healers spent much of their time.

The role of listener was one I had perfected long ago as a girl in Brooklyn with my grandmother. We had a private ritual that required certain conditions—her apartment being empty except for the two of us, her involvement in some methodical kitchen task, my placement at the kitchen table over my schoolbooks.

There was something about this scene—my position as a serious student on a clear table, unencumbered by the chores that had once stymied her own ambitions, had the effect of opening a door in her, ushering forth long stories of her own thwarted Italian girlhood and her frustrations as a bright girl.

Her tale had the predictable plot twist for her place and time—the farm door slammed in the face of her goals, shutting her in with domestic tasks that would prevent her from achieving the education she wanted.

I knew that her telling me these tales was of benefit to both of us, that she was passing something on to me—my heritage as girl of the Guarneri family—and that in her own intuitive way she was releasing old angers and frustrations, letting me know that what had been thwarted in her might now be nurtured in me.

And by heeding her, I felt that I was helping something inside her heal. This was a pact between us, the listener and the speaker. I was on my way to being an English major and was already attuned to the structure of stories—the plot, the climax —and I saw that the resolution of my grandmother's story, the great denouement, just might be me.

This listener role was one mightily discouraged during the rush of medical training. In every hospital where I worked, there was always someone dying alone—usually an elderly female —who was pining for someone to talk to and to whom I found myself gravitating. That is, until some supervisor pulled me away.

"If she's not yours, you can't spend the time" was the general refrain. The belief that a doctor's attention was a finite thing, like money in the bank, which might run out if you spent too much of it, was a common one.

Burned-out doctors were thrown up as cautionary models of what could happen if you cared too much.

The brisk surface approach was what was recommended. Gliding across the slick top layer of the clinical. Implicit in this advice was that you had to save deep emotions to spend on your own loved ones.

It was because of this that early on, I decided my patients would be my family.

The lure of listening began tugging at me again once I began to practice and saw the hunger of patients to be perceived as more than a list of numbers, the results of an echocardiogram or catheterization, but as a compilation of unique stories and experiences that would help me comprehend them if I would only take the time.

The night after Russ's visit, I was so keyed up I couldn't sleep.

I got up and turned on my computer and searched several Native American sites. In one article I read about *duyukta*—a Native American term for harmony and balance.

I read: "Separation within oneself, from one's family/ clan, one's community, from the earth—these are causes of disharmony and disease."[10]

I thought of Russ's fists, that stony face.

He was furious, I realized.

A once-strong, proud man, he'd lost all the old connections that had given his life meaning. He'd found himself diminished and alienated, in physical distress, with nowhere to go and no people to go to.

In the midst of a Western culture that stressed individuality over clan or community, Russ was adrift, divorced from the wisdom of his heritage.

Dead man walking, a silently furious man, rendered helpless by heart disease.

This was the theme of the story he'd told me.

Had I treated Russ earlier in my career, this might have been the end of our story, not the beginning. He would have been part of the assembly line of patients who had moved through my office, whose arteries I'd opened without teaching them how to open their lives and hearts.

Russ would have gone back to his apartment and continued his diet of pork, potatoes, and Coca-Cola. He would have continued bottling up his frustrations, and his vessels would have inexorably closed again.

I would have dealt with his heart and dutifully ignored the rest.

But I'd changed—my patients had changed me. They had shown me the importance of the heart's biography. They had taught me that coronary disease is physical, spiritual, and emotional. And that there could be a bridge between the conventional world of modern medicine and the type of healing known as alternative medicine.

The Healing Hearts Program that I directed at Scripps had been designed as that kind of bridge to help heart patients change their lives, and I wanted Russ to enter it.

At our next appointment, I told him, "I've done everything I can for you; now the ball's in your court. I need you to do everything you can to keep your arteries open. I need you to eat differently, exercise, decrease your weight, and learn ways to reduce your stress. But I also need you to think differently, to believe you will get well, to *want* to get well again."

I gave him the glossy brochure for our Healing Hearts Program, laid out at the foot of the Pacific. Customarily, this was all I had to show a patient for him to eagerly sign on. But Russ's reaction was contrary. As he leafed through the brochure, I saw the old shadows fall across his face.

"I don't know about this," he said.

"Why, what's the problem?"

"I'm just not sure."

"Russ . . ."

He looked up at me, and the shadows disappeared.

"I don't have enough money for a hotel room in La Jolla," he told me.

I looked past him out my office window at the ocean; as a displaced New Yorker, I still half expected to see a brick wall or a rubble-filled parking lot. The Pacific, right there in front of me, was still an unexpected thrill.

How far was I willing to go with this guy? I asked myself. Now that he was on the brink of real change, how much was I going to do?

The bonds and barriers between patient and doctor had been drilled into me since medical school.

My training told me that I was the doctor and Russ the patient, that he was sick and I was well, that I had the answers and he the questions. I'd been taught that the two of us should remain strictly apart, with me imparting wisdom and Russ the obedient and passive recipient.

But this arrangement wasn't working. I had learned as much from my patients as I'd ever gleaned from journal articles or textbooks, and it was not going to work by my being cool and detached and remaining on my side of some invisible barrier.

"I've got space in my house," I heard myself saying, to my own surprise, "You and your family can stay there."

That night I lay awake, agonizing over my decision, examining it from endless points of view. Would my colleagues find my behavior unprofessional? Would I feel uncomfortable having friends over with Russ and his family milling around? What if my dogs didn't like them?

My concerns were valid—it was a challenge having Russ and his family up close and personal during that first weekend in the heart program. I had to remind myself to be suitably dressed before wandering out to the kitchen or sashaying out of the shower. And even if I wanted to, I was no longer able to hide behind the authority of my white coat.

I was a regular woman now, standing in her kitchen, wearing her flip-flops, feeding her dogs, and making her salads. I had to hold my tongue when I saw Russ's son go out to their car to sneak in the bright red cans of Coke that his father was supposed to be avoiding. This was his path, not mine.

Russ benefited from all the components of our Healing Hearts Program, from yoga and meditation to vegetarian cooking classes, but the support groups and counseling were among the most important.

Our heart program couldn't provide Russ with his lost tribe, but the support group he entered may have been the next best option. I found myself hesitating by the glass doors to catch sight of his profile during these sessions. I couldn't tell what he was saying, only that he was saying it.

As I looked in at him, a verse from childhood Bible school floated into my head.

"Everything is shown up by being exposed to the light," St. Paul said, "and whatever is exposed to the light itself becomes light."

Research has documented the healing power of confiding in others. James W. Pennebaker's research on the correlation between suppressing our stories and illness, on the one hand, and telling our stories and increased health, on the other, is especially compelling and well researched.[11] As Russ himself later said: "Nothing got better for me until I began to talk about it."

Group support is a central part of Dean Ornish's heart disease reversal program, a model for ours. According to Ornish, not only do support groups help participants let down walls, express feelings, and learn to listen compassionately, but group members also motivate one another to sustain lifestyle changes, such as exercise, diet modification, and smoking cessation.[12]

In California, the shift from spring to summer is subtle but monumental, and during this period, something profound also shifted in Russ.

As he continued the program, his cholesterol and triglyceride levels improved, and for the first time in years he was able to walk without chest pain.

As his physical condition improved, I watched that tight, stoic face continue to soften as his suppressed anger finally emerged. Under his shell of toughness was a bruised, tender man, full of hurts and frustrations that he finally felt free to express.

Group counseling also changed the dynamic of his family life. Where Russ had once sat, ill and immobile, the center of the universe, there was suddenly movement again. He no longer needed to control his family through his heart disease, because it was no longer controlling him. His wife and son were unlocked from their static positions as protectors and guardians of his ill health.

His wife, in particular, who'd spent her days devoted to his care, had her life back. In counseling herself, she was now able to go out in the world without worrying that Russ would collapse at home. Their son even developed healthier eating habits and exhibited less fear that his father was going to die.

But the deepest indicators of Russ's success weren't his lowered cholesterol and triglyceride levels, but what I found him working on one afternoon—an intricate, many-threaded web with red beads woven into its center.

"What's this?" I asked him.

"A dreamcatcher, to ward off nightmares. We believe bad dreams become entangled in the sinews and threads. You hang it near where you sleep. This one's for you."

He handed it to me, and I held it up in my hand. And then I saw that the table behind me was covered with these intricate ornaments.

This creative side of Russ had been submerged deep under his illness; now his works of art hang throughout our offices at Scripps, a reminder of the great energy that had been locked inside.

Another day I entered one of the offices and found Russ sitting off in the corner with a young woman coworker.

"What's going on?" I asked the group leader.

"Russ is giving Gena a kokopelli."

"What's that?"

"For fertility—she's having a hard time getting pregnant. It's very powerful. Mary Jo and Dan claim he's already helped them conceive."

I backed out of the room—I wasn't exactly in the market to have my own fertility increased.

This is not to say that Russ's physical condition hasn't required continued medical intervention—it has. But now, seven stents and over seven years later, when I wake some nights worried about him, I see his dreamcatcher in the corner of my bedroom, and I remember that Russ advanced far beyond my technological fixes. He's found his own way.

Anthropologist David Maybury-Lewis says that individuals in a tribal society grow up in a defined world where people know their place and their relationship to others. In our modern Western culture, however, we grow up in a seemingly limitless world where we are often adrift and terribly alone.

I believe that this was what Russ's heart had been trying to tell him—that without community, clan, or a connection to his spirit, he and his heart were floundering.

As a spokesman for the medical technology company that helped fund our heart center, Russ has found a role that's helped keep him alive and vital nearly a decade after his doctors had given up on him.

He has stood in front of packed audiences across the country telling the story of how he lost his way, then found it again, one of the most ancient of tales.

And the audiences fulfill their part of the bargain. They give Russ what he wants—what we all want: They *listen*.

Chapter Five

The Landscape of Depression

In the second century, the physician Galen spoke of the heart's unusual physical properties, that as an organ, it is "hard flesh, not easily injured. In hardness, tension, general strength and resistance, the fibers of the heart far surpass all others."[1] Leonardo da Vinci, who drew illustrations of the heart during the Renaissance, also noted that "the heart is of such density that fire can scarcely damage it."[2]

Yet as the seat of our deepest feelings, the heart is, as we know, all too sensitive, registering through pains, pangs, flutters, and skips the thousand varieties of sufferings that Buddhists claim humans experience—from anger, jealousy, and fear to terror, shame, and, all too often, sadness.

Occasionally when I meet a new patient, I feel as if the fictional characters I studied as an undergraduate have come stepping out of the old books, transforming themselves into flesh. My depressed patient Jean, for example, could have been an older female version of those abandoned, loveless boys in Dickens—Pip or Oliver Twist—or perhaps even a tragic figure out of Shakespeare. With her hanging head, slouched figure, and woeful face, I wouldn't have been surprised to hear her utter: "Oh, God . . . how weary, stale, flat and unprofitable seem to me all the uses of this world."

Jean could have been a spokeswoman, a senator from our increasingly sad and lonely culture.

According to the World Health Organization, approximately 18.8 million American adults, or about 9.5 percent of the U.S. population age eighteen and older, in a given year, suffer a depressive disorder.[3] 25 percent of American households consist of one person living alone; 50 percent of marriages end in divorce, affecting more than a million children.[4]

And adjusting for population growth, ten times as many people in the Western nations today suffer from "unipolar" depression, or unremitting bad feelings without a specific cause, as did fifty years ago.[5]

When she arrived at my office, Jean possessed the constellation of symptoms that often coexist when depression and heart disease mix. At seventy-five, she was listless, overweight, and hopeless, moving through her days as if muffled by a blanket, burdened by the weight of the world. Behind her owlish glasses, her expression seemed permanently aggrieved and sour.

Because her blood vessels were small and severely diseased, she had been told by her other physicians that she not only was ineligible for a bypass but would likely die soon from coronary disease. This diagnosis, not surprisingly, had knocked her even further into the spiral of depression.

In America, we have a bias toward a pioneering, go-it-alone mentality, toward individualism and against interdependence of any kind. In another time, Jean's life might have been centered on work, family, or faith, but she had none of these to sustain her. She lived alone and, by her own admission, spent most of her days sitting in front of the television. She had moved a number of times and had no long-term connections. There was no mooring, no safety net, nothing bigger than herself to act as a counterweight when trouble entered her life.

I spent a long time interviewing Jean, but she seemed reluctant to reveal much about herself. She avoided my eyes and spoke so slowly that I had to keep myself from finishing her sentences.

She didn't have any questions for me, so I tried throwing some at her. "Yes," she said when I asked whether she considered herself depressed.

"How long have you felt this way?"

"Forever," she mumbled, looking at her feet.

"Has anything helped you?"

"Not for long."

I'd never met a more uncomfortable conversationalist. Still I persisted, hoping she'd crack open her door a bit and display anything that might be revealing.

"Do you have family anywhere, Jean?"

"A sister in New York. She cheated me out of my father's inheritance; I don't speak to her anymore."

"What else can you tell me about your background?"

She shrugged. "I was the last of five kids. Everyone was worn out by the time I came along. I didn't do well in school. I think I had what they call a learning disorder now. I married my husband to get out of the house, but he started fooling around the first year."

"Do you have any hobbies or interests?"

"Sometimes I play solitaire on my computer." She hesitated, and a slight blush colored her face. "And I guess you could say I'm hooked on the home shopping channel. I had to file for bankruptcy; I spent so much on my credit cards. I figured I'm dying soon, so who cares?"

"What did you buy?" I couldn't help asking.

"Clothes, costume jewelry."

I looked at her bland outfit—a pilled sweater vest and voluminous matching pants—and wondered what she had stockpiled in her apartment.

"Sometimes," she murmured, "I get all dressed up, but then I don't have anywhere to go."

By the time she left my office, I opened my window, as if to release the cloud of despair, the sad little atmosphere Jean seemed to carry with her.

Jean was fading away, and it was clear that her despair, apathy, and isolation were all linked with her coronary disease. Passive and victimized, she fit a profile I'd seen too many times. It wasn't always clear which had come first, the depression or the heart disease, but one thing was certain: These two conditions were joined in a seamless and deadly dance.

Jean was taking the selective serotonin reuptake inhibitors (SSRIs) that another doctor had previously prescribed for her, but it was abundantly clear that something deeper than her serotonin level was amiss.

These antidepressants couldn't address the underlying issue of her isolation and loneliness. How could this woman be as completely adrift as she seemed? And what could I really do about it? Adopt her? Fix her up? I was a cardiologist, not a matchmaker or a social director.

I was so busy that I was hardly the one to give advice on connecting with people. With my hectic schedule, I was finding it challenging to keep up with family and loved ones myself, to receive my own daily minimum requirement of love and affection. I hadn't married or had children so I could devote myself to my patients, but some nights, when I got home exhausted, I collapsed into a heap and switched on the *Antiques Roadshow* to hear some mild good news—for example, that a painting of kittens found in someone's attic was worth three thousand dollars.

In fact, with the intensity of our work, doctors are at high risk of becoming emotionally exhausted, burned out, and inconsolable themselves. Rates of alcoholism, drug addiction, and suicide are high.

I saw depressed and burned-out physicians all around me—their humor depleted, their enthusiasm and empathy long gone. I sometimes passed one of them, shuffling like a zombie through late-night hospital halls, with bloodshot eyes and a pallid face.

One of my patients was a top cancer surgeon who'd nearly collapsed during surgery from his own arterial blockages. Proud of his skill under pressure, he had finally had to call in another surgeon to help him finish the procedure.

Sitting at home, he grew increasingly morose.

But he couldn't let it go; nor would he move on to another type of doctoring.

"I'm a surgeon, that's it. . . . If I can't do that, what am I good for?"

I gave up; he wouldn't be comforted or advised.

Men often seem more susceptible to this kind of despair.

Take away their work, and you take away their reason for living, while women are more likely to find friends or take up hobbies to fill their time. But I was all too aware that depression, like heart disease, cut across gender, race, income, and class lines. It could easily grab any of us by the collar and drag us down.

Humans are tribal. We need one another. The heart program that I prescribed for Jean seemed to be just what she needed. Three days a week, her name was called in a roll call; people expected her, she became part of a clan.

"I'm so glad to see you here!" I said the first morning I found her near my office, and her face flushed a deep dark red—with pleasure, I hoped.

Given even the slightest attention or support, Jean thrived. She was plugged into a support network that called to remind her about healthy eating habits and even picked her up on the mornings of the program. I would glimpse her pedalling slowly and laboriously on the stationary bike when I came in most mornings, and sitting in group support sessions when I left for lunch. She still didn't seem to interact much with others, but her improvement was clear. A month into the program, she pulled out her waistband to show me all the weight she'd lost.

"That's great, Jean. How much?"

"Twelve pounds."

"Terrific. And how are the group sessions going?"

"All right. I don't think some of the people like me much. And my self-esteem's still not very good."

So she hadn't been completely altered. I knew not to hope for total miracles, just small daily ones.

Still, for Jean, with her low-key, chronically negative way, these results were pretty impressive.

But at the end of her program, when the strong support component ended, Jean was left to her own devices, and she collapsed back into her old ways. Without reinforcement, she stopped attending the voluntary exercise and group sessions.

Soon she disappeared like vapor back into the community —just another gray older woman, invisible again.

A social worker who went to visit Jean reported that she was holed up in her apartment, seriously depressed.

"She said she hasn't spoken to anyone for weeks. She didn't even want to talk to me."

I had my secretary call and ask Jean to come in for an appointment, but Jean declined. I wouldn't see her again until her next checkup, months away.

But during that period, I frequently thought of her and the complete self-focus of her sadness—the way she couldn't peer out of her deep well to see anything—or anyone—but herself.

In this and other ways, she fit the depression–heart disease profile that the expert James Lynch discusses in his research on loneliness—an unloved child, difficulty as a student, a blamer of others who found communication so difficult that she had retreated into herself. Lynch has spent decades studying how loneliness contributes to a markedly increased risk of developing premature coronary heart disease. "Mortality rates in the United States for all causes of death, and not just for heart disease, are consistently higher for divorced, single, and widowed individuals of both sexes and all races," he writes in *A Cry Unheard: New Insights into the Medical Consequences of Loneliness.*[6]

People have always suffered from depression and loneliness. But there is a factor in modern loneliness that, according to researchers like Lynch, is made worse by disruptions in family and community life. It's also been exacerbated by the replacement of face-to-face conversation with computers and other forms of electronic communication.

According to Lynch, people like Jean, who performed poorly in school and lacked love and were criticized at home, can find communication with others extremely difficult and may avoid it, repeating this pattern throughout their lives. For many depressed and lonely people, communication can be viewed as a threat, triggering the activation of the fight-or- flight response, the secretion of stress hormones that increases blood pressure and makes the heart beat faster. People experiencing this kind of anxiety are then more likely to withdraw from interaction with others and become more isolated. This can easily lead to depression.

On the other hand, face-to-face interaction that includes others, and is not viewed as threatening, has a healthful result, inducing a physiological state of relaxation.

Plenty of other research reinforces the link between depression and heart disease. In fact, depression stands beside high blood pressure and elevated cholesterol as a major risk factor for coronary artery disease. Those with heart disease who are depressed have an increased risk of death after a heart attack compared with those who are not depressed—four times as likely, in one study.[7] While about one in twenty American adults experiences major depression in a given year, the number goes to about one in three for people who have survived a heart attack.[8] Depression also seems to make it more difficult to take the needed medications and to carry out heart disease treatment.

At the University of Washington, an ongoing study found that factors such as depression, anxiety, a sense of self-efficacy, and the quality of spousal support were better predictors of a patient's degree of physical impairment than the severity of coronary artery disease, even when arteries were blocked as much as 70 percent.[9]

And according to the Harvard Mastery Study, a forty-two-year follow-up of students at Johns Hopkins University, the parent–child relationship in childhood proved to be a major predictor of major illness, including heart disease and cancer, in midlife.[10]

Why is depression so tough on the heart? Depression and anxiety disorders can increase blood pressure, affect heart rhythm, alter blood clotting, and lead to elevated insulin and cholesterol levels. These factors, along with obesity, form a cluster of signs and symptoms that often serve as predictors of heart disease. Depression may also result in chronically elevated levels of stress hormones, such as cortisol and adrenaline, which can elevate blood pressure, triglycerides, and LDL, or "bad" cholesterol.[11]

While researchers are still labouring to unlock the biochemical connections between depression and other disorders, one study of the neurobiological mechanism of depression has identified a condition called vascular depression caused by silent strokes deep within the brain's emotional centers. According to the principal investigator of the study, "This evidence suggests a two-way street, with risk factors for cardiovascular disease influencing the onset of depression in otherwise mentally healthy patients."[12]

As far as SSRIs are concerned, results of the Sertraline AntiDepressant Heart Attack Randomized Trial (SADHART) indicated that treatment with the SSRI sertraline (Zoloft) significantly improved mood among cardiac patients with a history of previous depression. But in patients who developed depression *after* a heart attack, there appeared to be no difference between SSRI treatment and a placebo.[13]

In addition, researchers had expected that a large percentage of patients would develop depression in the hospital after their heart attacks, that as a stressful event for vulnerable people, the heart attack would be the precipitating event. But instead, more than half of the cases of depression in the study began prior to hospitalization. According to Dr. Alexander Glass, of the New York State Psychiatric Institute, "Instead of saying the heart attack precipitates depression, it's just as easy to say that the depression precipitated the heart attack."[14]

Unfortunately, many families think, *Of course Grandma's depressed, she's got heart disease. Why shouldn't she be?*

This is a dangerous fallacy. Depression is *not* an inevitable side effect of cardiac disease. In fact, only 20 percent of those who sustain a heart attack become depressed.[15] Yet many families—and doctors—expect the cardiac patient to feel sad and don't realize that depression is a treatable disorder.

I didn't see Jean again until her next appointment three months later. By then she'd regained all her weight and was more depressed than ever, though heavily medicated by her psychiatrist. Her tests also indicated that her heart disease had progressed dramatically.

Jean didn't seem to care. She sat in my office, withdrawn and listless, staring out the window as I discussed her test results as if she were in another world.

Jean was fading away before my eyes. This might be my last chance to help her. But how could I crack open her tough heart? I doubted that more drugs or psychotherapy would help her. She had already had so much talk therapy that she could quite readily elucidate all her problems. In fact, her support group had provided her with an all-too-sympathetic venue when it came to rehashing and refocusing on the traumatic events of her childhood. When she stopped attending these meetings, she still remained preoccupied with her past. I realized that transforming Jean, deep in her seventies, into a cheerful person, willing to relate and listen to others, was going to be far too tall an order.

I sat down, scribbled three words on my prescription pad, and handed it to her. Jean peered at it, then adjusted her glasses.

"A small what?"

"Dog."

She stared at the paper another moment; then she looked up at me and did something I'd never seen before. She smiled.

I was to see a lot more of that in the following months. It turned out that in this arena, Jean was a total push-over, a complete marshmallow. The nine-pound terrier mix she adopted from the pound seemed to stand in for all she'd never had in her life—a companion, a child, a loyal friend.

During one visit, when she came to pick up a pre-scription and have her blood pressure taken, I almost jumped out of my skin when a small white head with a rhinestone collar appeared, panting, from the corner of her duffel bag.

"Alice, honey!" Jean was actually beaming.

In our culture, pets are often the only providers of unconditional love.

Her dog forced Jean to walk, to care about some-thing other than herself, to get out into nature, and to talk to other dog walkers she met. It gave her a context, a reason for being, a way to forget herself.

Animals have always played a major role in my own life. My poodle, Sam, has become one of the central loves of my current life, and I cleaved to our barreled-shaped, brown-and-white mutt, Dixie, during the painful years of my late adolescence. My grandmother came from a time and place where animals were meant for work, not companionship. She was outwardly gruff with Dixie and tried to keep her on the margin, training her to an inch of her life to remain on the linoleum-floored rooms of our apartment. But I noticed that it was also my grandmother who hand-fed Dixie homemade meatballs. And after my mother's death, my grandmother gave up the linoleum rule entirely and didn't say a word when I took Dixie into my room. So I was well aware of the value and companionship of animals, though I hadn't previously connected them with heart disease survival before.

Dr. James Lynch has also done pioneering research on the role animals play in social support and long-term survival of heart patients.

Lynch writes about a defining moment in his appreciation of the power of animal companions. While monitoring his ten-year-old daughter's blood pressure, he watched it fall by half when she began to stroke her beloved dog. Lynch had previously noted how the blood pressure of dogs and other animals was reduced when they were petted, but now he recognized that similar reactions occurred in humans.

In a landmark study of a group of heart patients over a number of years, Lynch was interested in discovering what determined long-term survival once patients were released from a coronary care unit. The most potent factor was the extent of heart damage. But the second most important variable was a surprise: Heart patients with pets had a far higher chance of living than those who didn't. In fact, *four times* more patients without pets died within the first year, even though they made up only 42 percent of the population he'd studied.[16]

Research suggests that the human need for love may be not just a matter of sentiment but an actual physical necessity. The limbic portions of the brain, where dreaming occurs and emotions arise, properly function only when a person feels love and connection.[17]

In one study of 149 men and women with angina who were questioned before catheterization about whether they felt loved and supported, those with the greatest perception of love and support displayed the smallest amount of coronary artery disease.[18]

But I wouldn't have needed any of these studies. Jean was proof enough. I saw for myself what love could do to a heart, let alone a face. I don't think I'd ever seen anyone so transformed. Within a month of adopting Alice, she'd lost weight and her depression seemed to have lessened. She and her little dog went everywhere together. She even obtained permission to bring Alice to the program with her and wait in a carrier while Jean did her exercises.

A few years later, when we performed another angiogram, we found that Jean's condition—and medical technology—had improved enough that she was now eligible for bypass.

I went to see her right before her surgery and found her sitting up in bed, staring at a photo. She flipped it toward me as I approached: The photo was of Alice sitting at the top of a flight of steps, looking for all the world as if she were smiling.

"To help keep me calm before the surgery, they told me to look at a photo of someone I love," Jean said.

"That ought to do it,"

I told her.

"I hope I get out within a week. The kennel lady says Alice's miserable without me. She won't eat or anything."

"Lovesick," I said teasingly

Jean looked at me seriously from behind her thick glasses. "Yes, that must be what it is. I think that's what it was with me, too."

When the attendants came and rolled her away for surgery, Jean's hand on top of the bedsheet was still clutching the photo of her dog.

Jean made me realize how less traditional approaches can play a crucial role in addressing the thorny problem of depression and heart disease.

Drug and cognitive therapy is not always the only—or even the best—approach for treatment. In fact, large randomized trials have indicated that the use of drug therapy and cognitive behavioral therapy to treat depression in heart disease patients doesn't improve survival in the depressed group.[19] It's not simply blocked arteries and muscle damage that affect a depressed heart patient's ability to survive and flourish. The heart's subtleties are equally important. And a growing body of research suggests that patients' hopes and beliefs can profoundly affect their prognosis.

Positive psychology, a field whose goal is to change the focus from what causes a troubled mind to what causes a happy one, contends that optimists are better off than pessimists. In heart disease, in particular, research has shown that optimism has been associated with a lowered risk of dying. In one study, patients who described themselves as highly optimistic had lower risks of all-cause death and lower rates of cardiovascular death than those with high levels of pessimism.[20] Research from the Harvard School of Public Health showed that optimism lowers the risk of heart disease in older men and that pessimism and hopelessness increase it.[21] And University of Pittsburgh researchers have reported that optimistic women demonstrate less thickening of the carotid artery walls.[22]

Not that being positive is simple or easy—it requires considerable effort. One way to cultivate it is by practicing gratitude.

Another contention of positive psychology is that those who are grateful for their blessings, and give thanks for their good fortune rather than dwelling on their misfortunes, are generally healthier and happier. Rather than their happiness making them grateful, it appears that being grateful has helped create their happiness.

Gratefulness has long been heralded as a virtue essential for health and well-being. Research now suggests that it also allows people to deal better with stress, causing them to be more optimistic, which seems to boost immune function.[23]

"If you want a strategy to increase your happiness, there's a lot out there that will help. You can take pharmaceuticals, but gratitude is something that doesn't have side effects," said Robert Emmons, a psychology professor at the University of California at Davis and part of one of the most widely cited gratitude studies.[24]

There's evidence that keeping a gratitude journal, a list of the things you have to be thankful for—even if you also include disappointments—helps keep what's positive in the forefront of your mind.

Writing the sentence *I am grateful for . . .* then recording your response in as much detail as possible can provide a sense of comfort and well-being as well as fostering positive thought and therefore health.

Finally, there's forgiveness.

Forgiveness has long been advocated by philosophers and religious leaders, from Buddha to Jesus. But science has been slow to verify the very real physiological burden of grudge bearing. Studies have shown that those who fail to forgive wrongs committed to them have more stress-related disorders and worse rates of cardiovascular disease than the population as a whole.[25] Researchers from the University of Wisconsin recruited thirty-six men with coronary artery disease and unresolved psychological stress related to domestic conflict, childhood, work, or war. Those who received forgiveness training showed improved blood flow to their heart muscle.[26]

Forgiveness seems to reduce the bitterness, anger, hatred, and fear that are part of grudge holding and that cause increased blood pressure and hormonal changes linked to cardiovascular disease and immune suppression.[27] In one study, researchers measured heart rates and sweat rates when subjects were asked to remember past slights and found that these rates increased, along with measurements of muscle tension.[28] Another examined twenty individuals in happy relationships and twenty in troubled relationships. The troubled group had higher baseline levels of cortisol, a hormone associated with impaired immune function—levels that increased even further when they were asked to think about their difficult relationships.[29]

Many of my depressed heart patients have been gnawing on the bones of past grievances for years. Jean was still blaming her parents for not loving her enough, her sister for cheating her out of her inheritance. But as Marianne Williamson says: "We are not held back by the love we didn't receive in the past, but by the love we're not extending in the present." [30]

Forgiveness, optimism, gratitude—these topics would have been dismissed as irrelevant when I was in medical school. Now they are increasingly subjects for serious scientific investigation, as much a part of the heart disease equation as blood cholesterol levels.

And there are times, as in the case of my patient Joe, when the most therapeutic thing I can do is simply to let his heart have its own way.

At seventy, Joe was short and round, with silvery blue eyes and a deceptively jolly air.

The first time I met him, he strolled into my office as if he'd known me all his life. "Good to meet you, Dr.

G.," he said, shaking my hand. "Do you know what the buffalo said when he dropped his boy off at school?"

"No, what?"

"Bi-son."

I groaned as he burst into raucous laughter. His wife, tiny and freckled, gave me the tolerant smile of the long married.

A displaced New Yorker like me, Joe was a retired stock-broker with a wide net of interests and friends. He had been an avid golfer, walker, and world traveler. But all that was in the past.

Joe's wisecracking disappeared when we talked about his heart disease. His other doctors had told him that his condition was so severe that there was little that could be done for him. His heart muscle was weakened from multiple heart attacks, his arteries were seriously blocked, and he wasn't strong enough to undergo bypass surgery. Nearly any exertion caused him to experience chest pain as well as exhaustion and breathlessness.

"They keep telling me to lose weight, but it's hard to slim down when you can't walk across the room without pain," he told me. "All I can do is sit in the chair and watch the world go by."

As a cardiologist, I'm well aware of issues of quality versus quantity of life. All you have to do is walk through the ICU to see plenty of quantity. It is hard to know when to stop. And, as far as I'm concerned, quality of life is just as important. What's the point of living longer if you are in pain or too depressed to get out of your chair? For me the issue is can I assist this person in getting back to enjoying a full life?

Joe's heart disease was severe enough that he'd had to curtail any activity that had ever given him pleasure.

Underneath his veneer of joviality, I began to suspect that he was, in fact, quite depressed. As our interview continued, his whole demeanour altered. He slouched in his chair, hung his head, and began enumerating a litany of vague complaints from listlessness to an inability to sleep. One of the most surprising features of depression in late life is that a patient may be as likely to say "My bones ache, I'm exhausted" as to say "I'm sad." Research on depression in the elderly has found that older people are less likely to say that they are sad than their younger counterparts.[31]

As a result, some patients may not present the emotional symptoms that are traditional signs of depression; rather, like Joe, they complain of exhaustion, aches and pains, or a lack of interest in food.

Depression is common after a heart attack and is associated with an increased risk of death for at least eighteen months afterward. One reason for this high mortality rate is that depressed patients are less likely to follow recommendations designed to reduce further cardiac events. This was the case with Joe, who had suffered three heart attacks in the past ten years. His wife said that after each attack, he had grown increasingly hopeless and more resistant to eating the healthy salad-

and-fish diet his doctor had recommended, or even taking his medicine.

"What's the use?" he told her. "Make me a hamburger. I might as well enjoy the little time I have left."

Trained to be tough and self-reliant, men often have a harder time than women admitting to depression, and Joe was no exception. "How can I be depressed?" he asked when I brought up the topic. "I've got a great wife, a roof over my head. When I was a kid we didn't know from one day to the next what we were going to eat or whether my father was going to keep his job. Now, that's a cause for depression!"

In a culture that equates maleness with being rugged and self-sufficient, this line of thought was one I'd heard before. But I firmly believed that Joe *was*, in fact, depressed, whether he recognized it or not.

I also had no doubt that he was nearing his last chapter. No doctor, including me, could tell him exactly how long he had left or what he should do with his remaining time.

I didn't plan to sugarcoat his situation or try to talk him out of his depression. As with Jean, I had to ask myself, What could I realistically do?

Looking again at his tests, I noted that all his arteries were totally blocked except for a single vessel, and in that I perceived a ray of hope.

"Joe, I want to ask you something. If you were healthy and could do whatever you wanted, what would you do?"

Joe's face brightened. "That's easy. I'd drive across the country and see my friends back east."

"Okay, I've got a plan."

As I outlined my idea to stent his single remaining artery and enroll him in our program to work on diet and exercise, his demeanour altered. He sat up, his head rose, and I saw a windowpane of light in the back of his blue eyes. We both knew that we were only buying him time, but in a sense, that's all we're ever doing. This plan at least gave him a goal.

Joe's stent insertion was a success and helped ease his chronic chest pain. Perhaps just as important, he immediately found a dozen new buddies in the heart program, an extended clan whom he could confide in and who shared the same physical challenges. Together they embarked on a gentle exercise program designed for heart patients with serious disease. Joe seemed to prefer the water exercise component. Soon I was able to tell the days when he was attending the program; all I had to do was follow the laughter to the pool area, where he sat at the pool's edge, patients circling around to listen to one of his salty stories. Watching him, I thought of an old saying a colleague once told me: The *I* in illness is isolation, and the crucial letters in wellness are *we*.

One day, months later, I stood on the lawn at Scripps and watched a man amble jauntily toward me. As he grew closer, I was astounded to see that it was Joe.

"I can't believe it. Look how far you walked! Do you have any pain?"

"Not a bit," he said, taking my arm and leading me across the lawn. "Listen, I got a story for you."

I suppressed a groan but let him tug me along.

"A lawyer visited a client who'd been put in prison for murder. He says: 'I've got some good news for you and some bad news.' And the prisoner says: 'Okay. Tell me the bad news first.' 'The bad news is that they found your blood all over the crime scene.' 'So what's the good news?' the prisoner asks. 'Your cholesterol is one seventy.'"

Joe stopped in his tracks and laughed so hard that I couldn't help but join him. He was his old self—but even more so, ten pounds thinner and smiling.

"I've got my trip back east all planned," he continued. "We're leaving Thursday, but I need to ask a favor. I'm going to a Halloween party in New York, and I want to go as a doctor. Could you get me scrubs to wear?"

"Of course," I said, "Come over tomorrow, and I'll get it together for you."

He arrived at my office the next day and collected a surgical gown, gloves, and a cap. I even threw in a stethoscope.

"You're *giving* me this?" he asked, holding it up.

"It's a loan." After giving me a hug, he stopped in the doorway. "Thanks, Dr. G. For everything."

"Have a ball." I watched him amble down the hall, joking with the doctors and flirting with the nurse. I thought that ill and old as he was, he had more life in him than anyone else in the place. Which is why I surprised myself by murmuring as he disappeared around the bend, "So long."

Three weeks later, I received a stat call from a hospital in Texas. It was Joe's wife, Liz.

"Joe died of a heart attack last night, Dr. Guarneri." She hesitated a moment, and I could hear her trying to gather herself. "I wanted you to know that he made it to the East Coast. He went to the Halloween party and got a chance to visit all his friends. He wore your outfit and he told everyone he was Dr. Feelgood. He was the life of the party. On the drive back home, he developed chest pain. . . ."

I couldn't speak for a moment, thinking of the sight of him walking away.

"No regrets. That's what Joe wanted me to tell you. He was able to say good-bye to all his friends. That's what he wanted. He wasn't sad. He wouldn't want you to be either."

"Thanks for letting me know."

"By the way, I found the gratitude list he'd written in his group sessions. I thought you'd like to know that you were number two on it, after me."

Depressions differ, as Joe and Jean illustrate. Jean's depression had most likely existed long before her illness and may even have precipitated it. Joe's, on the other hand, was probably situational, a result of his heart attacks, when he began grieving over the future he no longer had, as well as the limitations and curtailments caused by his disease.

After Liz hung up, I sat for a while in my office staring at a column of numbers in front of me. What was I even looking at? I couldn't remember. I put away my paperwork, turned off my computer, and walked down to the cafeteria. With its crowds and clamor, it was a place I usually avoided, opting to eat lunch alone in the quiet of my office.

I sat down with my soggy sandwich between two exhausted-looking residents, who began telling a gross joke I'd already heard several times before.

It was a bright day in La Jolla and thick buttery light filled the room, a slice of it falling across the table and up my arm, a golden slab. I savored its warmth along with my cup of coffee and watched my own plain hand obeying my neural order to lift and drink.

"How are you doing, Mimi?" one of the residents asked after a moment, and I made myself look up at him, meet his eyes, and smile in return.

"I'm good," I told the resident, and my eyes blurred with sudden liquid. It had been a long while since I had taken time to be aware of this, let alone feel grateful.

Thanks, Joe.

Chapter Six

Sacred Revelations

My first encounter with angels occurred when I was seventeen and working for the emergency ambulance corps in Brooklyn.

We'd picked up a middle-aged man named Lou Esposito who had collapsed from a heart attack at a social club in downtown Bensonhurst. It was a balmy Brooklyn night, and by the time we rushed the stretcher out of the club and into the ambulance, we had to push through a crowd of drinkers, lined up to get into the club.

This dramatic scene was one I'd learned to savour— the rush of adrenaline, the whirling lights, and the heroic sense that if you were swift and efficient enough, you just might save someone's life.

After we turned on the siren, I couldn't believe how usually belligerent New York drivers pulled aside, allowing us to barrel by in our lit mobile rescue capsule. This show of respect was beautiful to me, a sign of the unifying spirit of humanity in the face of disaster, one of the few times when we all banded together.

Lou Esposito was a well-known neighborhood character, a butcher by day and a bookie by night. I was used to seeing him behind the counter of his meat market, handling the demanding housewives who wanted their veal breast or bracciole sliced just so. Tonight he was dressed in his usual after-hours attire—gold chains, aviator sunglasses, and a knit shirt that we volunteers had unceremoniously reduced to shreds to get at his chest. As far as I knew, he wasn't the type for religious visions or visitations. But while we were struggling to get him hooked up to a heart monitor, he suddenly cried out: "Oh God! Look at that! There's an angel in here."

It was a testament to my scientific orientation that even at seventeen, I didn't turn around to peer in the direction he was gesturing but continued assisting my coworker, Mr. Gwynn, a placid, middle-aged man who was the epitome of blunt, cool efficiency.

As a Catholic, I'd been raised with angels—hazy creatures featured in hymns and hovering in the background of paintings —but that didn't mean I literally *believed* in them.

In the third grade, my friend Sara told me that she had a guardian angel who'd watched over her during her tonsil surgery. When I asked her to prove it, she became furious. "It's faith, Mimi, you can't prove everything." This was a retort I would hear many times in the following years.

But I was a literal-minded student who liked the controlled atmosphere of the laboratory and the certainty of science.

That night, as Lou Esposito continued to rant about the angel, Mr. Gwynn said, "Okay, Mr. Esposito, we'll take your angel along to the hospital with us," and he slammed the ambulance door shut.

The two of us sat over him during the trip to the hospital wearing the knowing looks of the levelheaded, certain there was no room in that ambulance for an angel or any other celestial creature.

It turned out my attitude that day was a perfect fit for the mentality I encountered once I entered medical school. I learned that physicians were leery of talking about the spiritual aspects of healing, grouping them with astrology and other dubious nonsciences. As soon as a patient walked through a hospital door, she was viewed as a bag of organs that could be scanned, biopsied, palpated, injected. Since the spirit, as well as the mind, were unseeable and amorphous, they were left for specialists in temples and parishes. If you couldn't grow it on a petri dish, see it under a microscope, or annotate it on a bill, it wasn't considered real.

One of my earliest teachers was a heavyset, chainsmoking cardiologist who swaggered into the examining room exuding a whiff of his last inhale. He was a do-as-I-say-not-as-I-do type of doctor: patronizing, impatient, and all-knowing. When one of our dying patients, a devout Catholic, asked him to stay when the priest arrived to perform special sacraments, he scoffed and left the room.

"All the rites in the world aren't going to do him any good," he commented once we were in the hall. It was clear he considered himself the god of the house; there was no need for any other.

Several years after I'd become a cardiologist myself, I was called in by another physician to consult on a new patient.

I found a pale and distraught forty-six-year-old man who had a totally occluded right coronary artery and had just suffered a heart attack. With his shoulder-length brown hair and narrow face, he had a haunting, archaic look, as if he'd come from another century. From the angiogram, it looked as if he'd benefit from a straightforward procedure—an angioplasty and maybe a coronary stent.

As I reviewed the chart, one sentence stood out in bold to me: The man was currently homeless. In fact, he'd fought with his sister and been asked to leave her home that very day. It was following this argument that he had developed chest pain and ultimately been taken to the hospital. He was unemployed, and there was almost no other information about him. I noticed that there was no sister, or anyone else, at his bedside.

I approached and introduced myself. "I'm Dr. Guarneri, and I'm here to fix your artery." I described the procedure, but I could tell he wasn't really listening. Instead, his eyes were glued on a spot just beyond my right shoulder.

"Doc," he said in a hoarse voice, "I've been seeing angels all morning. In fact, there's a tall one at the foot of my bed right now."

This time I couldn't help but turn around and follow his glance. Nothing, of course. Just the open door and the shiny hospital corridor.

Still this man's face was transfixed, like the face of saints in Renaissance paintings, full of recognition and certainty. A jolt went through me, and I thought of the incident in the ambulance with Mr. Esposito some twenty years before.

Between these two incidents was a world of experience. While my education had further assured me that my patient was hallucinating, possibly from a medication reaction, and that my job was simply to fix his artery, I was no longer the tidy sum of my textbook learning. I had looked down into the faces of more ill and dying people than I cared to remember. And the longer I worked as a doctor, the more I realized that in times of strife and illness, patients did not turn to their heart-lung machines or their physicians for meaning and comfort; they reached deep into themselves for their spiritual beliefs, for whatever it was that sustained them.

At these times, even the most hard-boiled and cynical patient displayed a yearning to believe in *something*. In fact, according to a survey by the National Center of Health Statistics, cardiologists asserted that *97 percent* of patients pray the night before they have heart surgery.[1] Although this didn't mean that I had applied any of this experience to myself, I'd come a long way in acknowledging that the spiritual connection that people feel to a force larger than themselves is a powerful one that cannot be underestimated or denied.

Given all this, it still wasn't clear exactly how I should respond to my homeless patient, who had shut his eyes now and was breathing deeply. Outside, I saw the resident pointing at her watch, a reminder that I had two other procedures scheduled that afternoon. No time for a discussion of celestial creatures.

"I need you to sign the consent form," I told him.

He opened his eyes and gazed over my shoulder. Then he took the pen, signed the form, and lay back again, exhausted.

"The angel's still here," he said. "Right behind you. There's a line of gold running along the edge of its wings." After a moment, he focused his gaze. "Do you believe me?"

Did I? Since we were alone, it was easier for me to give him the answer he clearly wanted. "Yes, I do," I said.

This seemed to ease him somewhat. "Good."

"What do you think it means—your seeing this angel?"

"It means I'm dying," he said, and then he closed his eyes again.

As I scrubbed my hands, I tried to wash this negative pronouncement from my mind. This procedure was not unlike hundreds I'd done in the past, and there was no cause for his fears to be valid. Certainly, there was always a chance of complications, but I saw no reason why I should be especially concerned. Still, it was a chilling prospect to work on a patient who believed he was not going to survive.

In spite of his dire words, the stent procedure went perfectly and without complication. The vessel was opened, a stent was inserted, and in twenty minutes there was a strong blood flow to his heart muscle. As was often the case, I felt reassured by the swift, clinical solution to this man's problem.

"Everything went well," I said to him when I entered the recovery area, realizing, even as I was doing it, that I had taken on a particularly brisk, doctorly tone. I patted his hand, but he seemed oddly unmoved by my cheerful words. In fact, he gave me an eerie, far-off nod, as if he were tuned in to some other channel.

Late in the day, when I went to see him again, he'd grown agitated. When I took his pulse, he grabbed my hand.

"The angels are back. I'm surrounded now. The smaller ones come and go, but that big one, at the end of the bed, stays with me all the time."

He was holding on to me for dear life, the veins in his forehead bulging. His pulse was racing, and he had a strange, ashen look. *What was going on?*

I turned to the fellow. "I want you to perform an echocardiogram of his heart."

The intern looked at me, his young face full of certainty and science. "Why? He's fine."

"Just do it, stat."

The ultrasound machine was rattled into the room, and my patient was hooked up so that we could view his living heart on a small-screen monitor. As the technician placed the probe on his chest, we watched in disbelief as his heart muscle, weakened from the heart attack, ruptured in front of our eyes. At that moment, the patient strained upward, half out of the bed, toward the spot where he'd been gazing all day.

The fellow said, "God, what's happening?"

I started to reply but then stopped myself. What could I say?

"Get him into surgery. Call Dr. Rico." I tried to sound authoritative, but I had goose bumps up and down my arms.

Despite emergency surgery and the most sophisticated, high-tech procedures, my patient died that night.

When the intern came to tell me the news, I acted surprised, but I wasn't. I'd known it was too late, and my patient had known it, too. I sat up reviewing his records, but it was just to keep myself busy. What I was really wondering about was how his sister felt after she heard the news.

As for me, I began paying attention to angels.

In fact, this experience had such a profound effect that I decided to do some exploring in order to find out whether there was any science of spirituality and sacredness. Surely, in this most esoteric of areas, there wouldn't be the kind of compelling research that I usually turned to for validation, but I was wrong. The attempt to quantify and analyse the spiritual dimension of health as well as the efficacy of prayer has become a growing field. Prayer, in particular, seems to have moved center stage in Western medicine.

From 1999 to 2003, the National Institute of Health's Center for Complementary and Alternative Medicine has more than doubled the dollars spent on research on religion, spirituality, and meditation. More than a quarter of all research funds for mind-body research goes into studying how religion, spirituality, and meditation affect people.[2]

As a Duke cardiologist, Mitchell Krucoff, says: "The first time you see a nontraditional practitioner take away chest pain or put a patient in agony to rest, or interrupt a heart attack without adding another drug or device at the bedside, you say, 'Nice coincidence.' The second time, you say, 'this is interesting.' By the third time, you say, 'we need to study this.'"[3]

Like me, Dr. Larry Dossey, a well-known authority on spiritual healing, had deep roots in the conventional Western scientific model. An internist who'd grown up in a religious environment in Texas, he'd turned his back on spirituality when he entered medical school.

But Western medicine couldn't explain the patients Dr. Dossey encountered who were blessed by so-called miracle cures—patients with terrible illnesses who were improved with prayer. One of the most impressive was the remission of a man with terminal lung cancer, who'd received no medical treatment but had members of his church congregation praying for him continually.

Dossey didn't take these cases seriously, however, until he discovered the existence of scientific studies that validated the health effects of prayer and devotion—the same type of impressive studies I began to discover.

"Almost all physicians possess a lavish list of strange happenings unexplainable by normal science," says Dr.

Dossey. "A tally of these events would demonstrate, I am convinced, that medical science not only has not had the last word, it has hardly had the first word on how the world works, especially when the mind is involved."[4]

Landmark research includes Dr. Elisabeth Targ and colleagues' 1998 study of the effects of prayer (or "distant healing") on patients who were suffering from advanced AIDS. After six months, those who received prayer survived in larger numbers, grew ill less frequently, and recovered more swiftly than those who received no prayer.[5]

Another is Dr. Randolph Byrd's 1988 study at the San Francisco General Hospital on chest-pain and heart attack patients. Researchers found that those who received prayer were clinically better than those who did not—meaning they had fewer complications, less need for antibiotics, and were less likely to develop pulmonary edema.[6]

But my favourite is Dr. Mitchell Krucoff's research at Duke University Medical Center, studying the effect of prayer on cardiac patients undergoing angioplasty and catheterization. Cardiologist Krucoff and nurse practitioner Suzanne Crater were inspired by a visit they made to a hospital in India that was run by Sri Sathya Sai Baba, worshiped by his followers as an avatar, an incarnation of divinity. The researchers were impressed by the upbeat atmosphere at the hospital following the daily visits of Sai Baba, so unlike the bleak and frightening feeling they'd so often encountered in Western hospitals.

"God came every day and made rounds and touched them," Krucoff says. "That kind of atmosphere has got to have physiological impact."[7]

Upon returning to the United States, the two decided to set up a pilot study of 150 patients at Duke University and Durham Veterans Affairs Medical Center to test the idea that spiritual influences could have a measurable impact.

Angioplasty patients were prayed for simultaneously by different religious sects around the world—from Buddhists in Nepal to Carmelite nuns in Baltimore to Baptists in North Carolina. The parishioners were asked to pray for the patients who were assigned to them, according to their normal customs. The researchers utilized a monitoring technique to follow patients from precatheterization to postangioplasty, tracking such items as stroke, heart attack incidence, and mortality. Those patients who were prayed for had fewer adverse outcomes than patients in the standard therapy group.

All these studies were double-blind, meaning that neither the staff nor the patients knew of their treatment. Because of this, it's difficult for skeptics to invalidate them by stating that any observed result of prayer must be due to the subject's expectation or the power of his or her beliefs.

And then there was the early research by Dr. Franklin Loehr, a Presbyterian minister and scientist, who even documented the tangible effects of prayer on microorganisms and plants.

In experiments conducted on germinating seeds, Loehr used three pans of various kinds of seeds. One served as the control; another received positive prayer and another negative prayer. The results regularly showed that prayer helped speed the germination of seeds and produced more vigorous plants, while negative prayer halted the germination of certain plants and suppressed growth in others.[8]

These studies are particularly impressive since it was impossible to charge that plants or microorganisms had been affected by positive thinking, suggestion, or the placebo effect.

It appears that prayer is something many people do for strength, hope, comfort, and guidance, but that few talk about.

As Professor Rodney Stark of Baylor University says, prayer is "one of the most common and unacknowledged activities on the planet."[9]

A recent Roper poll states that half of all Americans claim to pray or meditate daily, more than claim to attend religious services.[10] The Internet reverberates with prayer groups and networks, including the Internet site Beliefnet, a multifaith e-community, which report tens of thousands of prayer circles.

Some researchers speculate that prayer can lead to enhanced changes in the cardiovascular system by inducing a therapeutic state of calmness. One study used radioactive tracers and high-tech imaging techniques to peek into the different regions of the brains of Tibetan monks and Franciscan nuns during meditation. The research documented alteration in the activity of the brain along with blood-flow changes during meditation and prayer. "This could be the link between religion and health benefits such as lower blood pressure, lower heart rate, decreased anxiety, and an enhanced sense of wellbeing," says Dr. Andy Newberg of the University of Pennsylvania, author of the study.[11]

Some kind of religious belief or connection may also be helpful to the healing interaction between patients and doctors.

A number of small studies reviewed in *The Journal of the American Medical Association* found that many patients want physicians to consider their spiritual needs. In one study, 48 percent of the patients interviewed wanted their physicians to pray with them.[12]

And a study published in the journal *Oncology* found that medical personnel at a cancer center in New York City who described themselves as religious were less subject than other practitioners to emotional exhaustion or "diminished empathy."[13]

Researcher and author Herbert Benson found that people who regularly evoked a meditative state that he named the Relaxation Response felt increased spirituality and the presence of God or a higher power. This state is the opposite of the fight-or-flight response, which is linked with cardiac arrhythmia, depression, anxiety, and insomnia.[14]

In order to reach this Relaxation Response, two things are required, according to Benson: repetition of a prayer or thought or word and the return to this repetition if other intrusive thoughts arise. This is a scientific description of what is, in fact, ancient practice, common throughout many different religions throughout time. Focussed breathing and the repetition of prayers and chants can be found in early Christianity, Confucianism, and Jewish mysticism. Islam, Hinduism, and Buddhism weave ritual prayer into the daily routines of life.

Yet even as I read the research, I realized that science could never answer all the questions we ask about religious experience, nor should it. Intuition and faith are still the cornerstone of most spiritual practices, not empirical data. There is so much in medicine that is beyond our understanding. We don't fully understand why certain beta-blockers and antidepressants work the way they do—but that doesn't keep us from utilizing them all the same.

Why should it be any different with prayer and spirituality—which have thousands of years of human history behind them?

Still, it wasn't until my experience with my patient Milly that the spiritual dimension of healing actually pierced my own life.

It was three days before Christmas when Milly came into the cardiology clinic for a routine appointment.

At sixty-seven, she was a church organist and a deeply religious woman who'd spent much of her life ministering to children with cerebral palsy. Tall and stately, with a profile that reminded me of Eleanor Roosevelt, she'd been suffering for years from a cardiac arrhythmia called atrial fibrillation, which had been particularly resistant to treatment.

Atrial fibrillation, a chaotic, irregular rhythm arising from the upper chambers of the heart, is the most common of heart arrhythmias. For many patients, the underlying cause is high blood pressure or electrolyte abnormalities, such as low magnesium or low potassium. For others, it may be related to an overactive thyroid, coronary artery disease, or, as in Milly's case, a weak heart muscle. Atrial fibrillation is an unsettling condition that can cause a person to be keenly aware of each heartbeat. As Milly described it, "I feel like I have butterflies in my chest."

Other physical symptoms are even more bothersome: shortness of breath, sweating, chest discomfort, dizziness, fainting, and extreme fatigue. Milly had experienced them all. Medication certainly helped, but had not alleviated all of them.

Over her last several visits, I'd had the distressing experience of witnessing her profound physical decline. Her heart muscle was becoming progressively weaker, she was increasingly short of breath, and her legs were hugely swollen.

She must have known how dire her condition was, but she never showed it. Her manner remained warm and appreciative. In fact, she had recently stepped up the maternal interest she'd always taken in me, urging me to come over to her house for dinner and trying, through various ploys, to get me to attend her church.

"There'd be so many people there who'd love to meet you," she'd said on her last visit. "Sister Cecilia over at the parish is setting up a clinic for immigrants. She'd be so pleased to get your input. And Father Walsh is talking this week about the heart as a religious symbol—right up your alley."

As I had done many times in the past, I thanked her, but never had time to follow up on her invitation.

At our visit that day, I was stunned by Milly's condition—not by her decline but by her improvement. Her support-hosed legs in the wheelchair were so much less swollen that they looked as if they belonged to someone else.

"Your legs aren't swollen," I announced, bending down to touch them. I couldn't believe my eyes. "Did you change your medication?"

"No, dear. I'm taking everything the same as always."

I continued my examination, leaning over to listen to her heart with my stethoscope, catching her distinctive scent of Cashmere Bouquet.

"Milly," I said after a minute, "your heart's in regular rhythm."

"I know, dear," she said.

I looked at her. She had a special gleam in her eye. "In all these years; I've *never* heard you in regular rhythm. What are you doing differently?"

She shrugged. "Nothing. By the way, what are you doing New Year's? I'm making leg of lamb with fresh garlic and sage if you want to come by."

"I'm a vegetarian, but thanks." I was thrilled that she seemed so much better, but I didn't like being unable to figure out why. "I'm going to order an ECG, then I'll come back in to talk to you."

Sure enough, the ECG verified her regular rhythm. I wasn't sure why I needed the machine to tell me what my ear knew, but still it was verification.

"Okay, you haven't changed your medicine or anything, so now I'm completely stumped," I said when I came back into the room. "What did you do?"

As I asked the question, Milly shifted her head, and light from the window glinted on the gold cross she always wore around her neck. She was reluctant to remove it, so I had many close encounters staring at it while I noted her rapid and chaotic heart rhythm, sometimes as fast as 150 beats per minute.

Before I could think about it, I asked, "Did you go to a faith-healing service?"

Milly gave me an even look.

"You *did*? You went to a faith healer?"

"Well, not a faith healer exactly. He was an ordained minister. I thought you would laugh, so I didn't say anything."

"Tell me."

"Well, a friend of mine attends a church where this minister was coming for a special service. She was taking her daughter who has cancer, so I decided to go along. The healer was an older fellow with a cane, just a regular white-haired guy. He got up front and said, 'I want you to remember that any healing that takes place here tonight doesn't come from me, but it's a power that comes through me from the Holy Spirit.'"

"I watched a line of people go up front and kneel at the altar and receive a private moment with him. He didn't do anything very dramatic, just placed his hand over an area, or sometimes on it. Anyhow, after my friend and her daughter sat down, she whispered, 'You should go up, too.' So I decided *why not*? They started to push me up. The closer we came, I got more nervous. This isn't like me, you know, calling attention to myself. But there was no turning back. The line was short now, and it only took a few minutes before he came to me. He gazed straight into my eyes, and I didn't even have to tell him what was ailing me. As soon as he looked at me, he said, 'Your heart.' Then he placed his hand right on top of my head, and I felt an electric shock travel right through me. It was incredible."

"When was this?"

"A week ago."

As I listened to Milly, it occurred to me that we often deploy a treatment called cardioversion to treat atrial fibrillation or atrial flutter. In this technique, a special machine is used to send electrical energy to the heart muscle to restore normal rhythm. Could some version of this be what had happened to Milly?

I couldn't quite believe it. And I couldn't keep myself from bending down with my stethoscope to listen to her heart again. But what was I listening for? Some secret, some evidence that would finally explain to me what had occurred?

Staring at Millie's cross, I flashed back to an afternoon in Brooklyn that I hadn't thought about in years. My older brother, age ten, had been stricken with acute kidney failure. My maternal grandmother and a flock of ladies from her church had crowded into his small bedroom to sit vigil and say the Rosary.

I peeked in at them, gathered in a circle in their floral housedresses, heard the low sound of their murmuring and the muted clicking of their beads. The room smelled hot and pungent with the scent of candle wax and sweat. I felt as if I were peering in at some ancient ritual and quickly retreated before they could pull me in.

But I never connected my brother's eventual recovery, without dialysis, to these prayer sessions, which had continued for many weeks.

Nor did I give a second thought to the prayer cards and novenas that were so common in my neighborhood, though a particularly poetic line from one of them—"O Blessed Rosary of Mary, sweet chain which unites us to God"—remained in my memory for years.

Novenas, nine-day periods of prayer to obtain special graces or to make special petitions, were favourites of local women, who seemed to be frequently visited by urgent needs and sorrows. There were Little Flower novenas, Our Lady of Sorrows novenas. The women on our street were always praying desperately for something—the departure of an illness or the return of a husband. But as far I was concerned, this was a sign of their powerlessness, hopelessly old-fashioned and as superstitious as the lottery.

Finally, I had never given much weight to my aunt Rose's prayers for my future or to my aunt Gina's devotion to the sacred heart of Jesus. Aunt Gina had dreamed of entering a convent but ended up working instead in the church gift shop because her father hadn't wanted her to become a nun. She'd always tried to instill in me her own brand of piety and optimism.

"Mimi, ask the sacred heart for guidance," she'd implore me. "He is the divine physician."

And while I'd dutifully repeat the words "Sacred heart of Jesus, guide my course in life"—at least while she was standing there—I questioned whether any of this might make a real difference.

Or perhaps I should say that I'd never considered these possibilities until now.

An overwhelming memory of the prayers of the women of my family, transposed over space and time, fell over me like a wash of light. I opened my eyes to the present, to my white coat and diploma-filled wall, and the regular *lub-dub* of the beat in my ear.

I thought I'd finally discerned what Milly's heart, with its beautiful, regular rhythm, was trying to tell me.

Spiritual practitioners, from Buddhists to shamans, share the common goal of opening the human heart, but I, the expert in this region, had managed to keep mine closed to this dimension.

It took patients like Milly to make me realize that spirituality is a belief in a force greater than one's self that can encompass an array of beliefs without being embodied in an organized religion.

It has as much to do with how you live your life and treat others as the strict and punitive codes of behavior I had turned away from in my youth.

After my experience with Milly, I began to view cardiac procedures not just as everyday occurrences but as sacred ones. While catheterizations and angioplasties are overwhelmingly safe, there's no mitigating the fact that a tube is being threaded into a beating heart. And so now we prepare our patients in ways that were never taught in medical school.

With our use of guided-imagery tapes and CDs, patients often enter these procedures fantasizing about sunny beaches instead of IVs. With a background of calming music, these tapes lead them into visualizing serene, beautiful surroundings with a loved one beside them. Patients are encouraged to turn their thoughts away from anxiety and fear and to visualize themselves in the operating room, successfully undergoing the surgery with little pain.

"It's like a directed, deliberate daydream," says Diane Tusek, R.N., of the Cleveland Clinic Foundation. Tusek's research has demonstrated how this simple intervention does far more than bring calm. It also alleviates pain—subjects in one study required almost half the amount of pain medication as the control group—and reduces the length of hospital stay.[15]

And we also offer another special practice. For those patients who request it, we usher in a group of men and women who've previously undergone the procedure themselves. They gather around the bed, form a circle, join hands, and bow their heads. And then they do something that there is no manual for, no small print or AMA guidelines, no line charge on any invoice: They pray.

"I decided that not using prayer on behalf of my patients was the equivalent of withholding a needed medication or surgical procedure," Dr. Larry Dossey says, and I've come to agree.[16]

And that's why you'll find me there as part of the circle, the formerly reluctant physician whose armour of resistance now lies in a heap on the operating-room floor.

Chapter Seven

The Persistence of Grief

One of the many things I didn't learn in medical school is that it's possible to die of a broken heart. I've yet to see grief listed as the cause of death on a death certificate, but that's not because it doesn't happen.

This isn't the stuff of folk songs or romantic fiction. We've all known real-life couples who've died within weeks, months, or even days of each other, of friends and relatives who've languished after the loss of a loved one. There are scores of anecdotal cases—a Wisconsin couple, married for seventy-two years, who died within hours of each other in 1997; an elderly woman with normal coronary arteries who opened her door to the news of her husband's death in an auto accident, suffered a heart attack, and died on the spot.[1]

And there are more famous cases: Even though official records indicate that Johnny Cash died of complications from diabetes, many fans believe that he succumbed to a broken heart, just three months after his wife, June Cash, died of complications from heart surgery.[2]

We are not even surprised by these stories because we understand intuitively a truth that modern science now bears out. In a landmark 1996 study, Harvard researchers added grief surrounding the death of a significant person to a list of triggers that increase the likelihood of suffering a heart attack. Over a four-year period, 1,774 people were interviewed within a week after suffering an acute myocardial infarction. They were asked, among other things, "During the past year did you hear news of the death of a friend, relative or someone who was very significant in your life?"

A significant relationship to the antecedent death of a loved one was found in the data. The elevated risk of a heart attack in the first twenty-four hours after the loss of a loved one was fourteen times higher than normal; in the second twenty-four hours, eight times higher; and in the third twenty four hours, six times higher.[3]

Of all heart stories, tales of grief are most deeply etched in patients' psyches. But these losses are often buried—wounds that patients are unwilling to reveal.

When a trim, fit man in his forties arrived in my office one afternoon, wearing jogging shorts, I thought that he'd come to the wrong office.

I was indeed expecting a new patient and had spent the previous hour studying the voluminous pile of his tests, all showing the same thing: substantial blockage in two coronary arteries. As I leafed through the test results, I'd created a vision of this person in spite of myself, as someone sluggish and out of shape. But the man standing in my office doorway looked to be in better condition than I was, with muscled legs and a lean, tan physique.

"I'm Ken Rafle," he said, shaking my hand.

It was my new patient, all right.

"How far'd you jog to get here?"

"Oh, not far—about fifteen miles . . ." I couldn't take my eyes off him—he looked like he belonged in a vitamin advertisement.

The two of us continued the kind of banter we might have exchanged at a cocktail party—where the best hiking trails were and the best swimming beaches. Ken seemed eager to convey to me his impressive physical prowess in spite of his medical problems. But during a lull in the conversation, I brought my focus back to the sobering test results that lay before me on my desk.

Every disease has a narrative behind it, often a surprising one; the challenge is to find a way for the patient to lift the veil and reveal it—not only to the physician, but sometimes to himself.

"Let's talk about your heart," I said to Ken, and he cheerfully switched gears, without missing a beat. In fact, throughout our interview, he was relentlessly upbeat, showing me his square, white teeth in a smile that never quite seemed to reach his eyes.

"Well, basically my other doctors think I should have a bypass, or at least stents and drugs, but I don't want to go that route. I've decided to try and heal myself without surgery, using natural remedies and diet."

"Okay, let's hear what you've been doing."

"I started out by going on a cleansing fast, and since then I've been on a strict vegetarian diet . . ."

It turned out that Ken was nearly a poster child for everything I'd come to advocate over the years—and then some. He was a low-fat, no-sugar vegetarian, a regular exerciser, and a taker of fish oil and other heart-healthy supplements.

For the next ten minutes, he presented his impressive lifestyle changes to me as if he were making a Power-Point presentation. Yet for all his efforts—all the tofu, cholesterol monitoring, and fasting—he still hadn't been able to reverse his heart disease.

The more he talked, the more difficult I found it to reconcile the Ken who was sitting before me with the person with occluded vessels presented in my files. He seemed almost too perfect—too fit and agreeable. I was struck by the discrepancy between his healthy exterior and his interior of blockage and disease.

And there were other aspects of him I found interesting. During my examination, his chest area felt tense, rigid, as if he were coiled tight. His breathing was extremely shallow. When I asked him to inhale for me, it was as if he were expanding only a fraction of his lungs.

As I reviewed his test results with him, I noted that his blood pressure was high, which was at odds with his laid-back persona. When I touched his arm, he flinched, and for a second I glimpsed something else beneath the sunny facade—a frightened, skittish man.

"Is there any particular stress or burden in your life right now?"

"Not really," he said, averting his eyes.

I looked down at his chart again. His personal data were unremarkable. He was an executive in a local publishing firm, Jewish, married for a decade.

"Any children?"

He smiled. "Just a dog."

"Okay, I'm going to prescribe blood pressure medication, and I would like you to speak with my associate Rauni about our Healing Hearts program; otherwise, you seem to be doing everything right."

For the first time, Ken's face grew troubled. Clearly he had hoped for something more.

"What do you think about the new heart scans I've been reading about? Would that give us some information we don't have yet?"

The heart scan was probably the only test Ken *hadn't* had—he'd undergone every other possible diagnostic procedure, a few several times. The scan he was referring to passes X-rays through the heart, then transmits the data to a computer that forms an image. Unlike an angiogram, which picks up an image of blood flow through the vessel, these scans illuminate every detail inside and out. As a noninvasive diagnostic tool, the scan has some benefits over an angiogram, which requires sedation and a catheter threaded from the femoral artery in the groin to the heart.

But the point was irrelevant in Ken's case; he'd undergone angiography recently.

"We've already got good data on the location and size of your blockages," I told him. "An additional angiogram would not add anything new."

"How about my blood work? Can we review it again?"

I looked down at his numbers. "Well, your lipids are perfect; your triglycerides and cholesterol are good; so is your homocysteine level."

"What do you think of my C-reactive protein?" he asked, referring to a marker for inflammation that has been found to be an important culprit in causing heart attacks and strokes. This number was normal also.

"Do you have any other questions?"

Ken thought a moment, then shook his head as he stood to go.

Although I sensed that there was some further issue underlying his heart disease, he obviously wasn't going to reveal it to me, and I was hard-pressed to see what else I could do for him. Watching Ken leave, I thought that as much as technology attempts to weigh and measure us, humans harbour pockets of pain, wounds and tender spots that do not show up on routine tests. The causes of coronary disease are not always easy to quantify. Patients and physicians often find it easier to grasp concepts of blood pressure elevation and arterial narrowing than hazier areas of emotions, feelings, and grief. As many as half of the coronary disease cases cannot be linked to the usual suspects: traditional risk factors of family history, smoking, high blood pressure, obesity, and inactivity.[4]

Even cholesterol, a prime determinant of coronary disease, has long been known to be only one piece of a much more complex picture. This was one of the main findings of the thirty-year Framingham study, begun in 1948 and involving 5,127 people aged thirty to sixty-two. Every two years, these participants, who showed no signs of heart disease, underwent a complete physical examination. When you look at Framingham, you see that 35 percent of coronary disease occurred in people with cholesterol levels between 150 and 200. Framingham also found that 80 percent of people who had a heart attack had the *same cholesterol levels* as those who did not. Today we know that inflammation, small dense LDL, lipoprotein (a), and low HDL 2B are equally important.[5]

It's the same complex picture when it comes to family history.

I tell patients who are concerned about heart disease in their family that it's not just their genetic history that's crucial but the environment washing over their genes. Studies of identical twins who've been adopted and gone on to develop different illnesses in later life prove that it is as much the environment they were raised in as their genetic predisposition that affects their future health.[6] Predisposition isn't destiny.

The next week, I was surprised when Rauni called and wanted to talk more about Ken.

"You didn't tell me your patient was such a time bomb," she said.

"What do you mean?"

"When I questioned him about being two hours late for his appointment, he completely broke down."

"You're kidding. Why?"

And it was then, through Rauni, that I finally learned the true story of Ken's heart.

Even though he hadn't admitted this to me, Ken and his wife, Cindy, had once had a son, George, an only child, who'd been long planned for and much loved.

When the couple had married in middle age, they had been desperate to have a family, but Cindy had had difficulty conceiving. The couple had undergone years of fertility treatments, with Cindy miscarrying twice before becoming pregnant with George. It had been a difficult pregnancy, and the boy had been born with a lung ailment that required long hospital stays and constant monitoring through his first few years. Finally, when he was four years old, the doctors pronounced him cured. The couple was ecstatic; George was the product of their deep love, mutual dedication, and commitment, and they doted on him.

On George's seventh birthday, he was trying out a pair of Rollerblades that he'd been given by his grandparents. His skating was relegated to the family's long sloping driveway, where his parents could keep an eye on him. They tried not to be overprotective, but with his history, Cindy, in particular, had a hard time granting him independence. After several minutes of watching him, Ken had gone inside to make a phone call, leaving Cindy alone on the front steps.

George skated up and down the driveway for another few minutes while Cindy wandered over to the side of the house to look at a tree that had recently been planted.

During the few seconds of Cindy's distraction, George reached the end of their driveway and bent down in the street to readjust his Rollerblades. In the time it had taken Cindy to walk twenty yards, her son was hit by a car.

Looking out the window, Ken saw what happened and ran outside.

In spite of his wife's pleas that they wait for an ambulance, he picked George up in his arms, put him in the family car, and drove him to the emergency room.

There, he and Cindy sat for four days and nights, dressed in the same clothes, barely eating or sleeping, watching their son fade away. There were prayer circles, specialists called from nearby cities. There were blood transfusions and plans for surgery, but in the end, there was no way to save him.

After George died, everything in the couple's life collapsed.

It's not unusual for parents to grieve differently. This was the case with Ken and Cindy. Cindy wanted to talk about George, to look at pictures, to commemorate and remember him. Ken, however, didn't want to be reminded. He refused to grieve or express his feelings and behaved as if George had never existed. He wouldn't go into his son's room or even walk up to the second floor, where it was located. Instead he threw himself into hiking and rock climbing in the mountains near their home.

It was during one of these hikes that he first developed angina, a tightness in his chest when he ascended a hill. He told himself it was nothing, but Cindy made him see a physician. Even though he'd had no history of heart disease or any other physical risk factors, Ken had developed significant blockage.

I was the last of a long line of physicians Ken had visited, hoping for an easy fix or magic bullet and never mentioning the death of his son.

I thought back to my question: Do you have any children? *Just a dog*, Ken had replied. I might have known. People rarely mention when they've lost a child. It's as if they have to block it out in order to survive.

This, I now saw, was the great tension I'd felt in Ken; at great cost and with considerable effort, he had walled off his wounded heart.

Ken's experience made me think of the story of Krisha Gotami, a young woman who lived at the time of the Buddha. When her firstborn child was about an year old, he fell ill and died. Grief-stricken and clutching his body, Krisha Gotami roamed the streets, begging anyone she met for a medicine that could restore her child to life. Some ignored her, some laughed at her, but finally she met a man who told her that only Buddha could perform the miracle she was seeking.

So she went to the Buddha, placed the body of her child at his feet, and told him her story. The Buddha listened with compassion, then said to her, "There is only one way to heal your affliction. Travel down to the city and bring me back a mustard seed from any house in which there has never been a death."

Krisha Gotami felt elated and set off at once. She stopped at the first house she came to and said, "I have been told by the Buddha to fetch a mustard seed from a house that has never known death."

"Many people have died in this house," she was told. She went on to the next house. "There have been countless deaths in our family," they said. And so on, until she had been all round the city and realized that the Buddha's condition could not be fulfilled.

She took the body of her child to the burial ground and said good-bye to him for the final time, then returned to the Buddha.

"Did you bring the mustard seed?" he asked.

"No," she said. "I am beginning to understand the lesson you are trying to teach me. Grief made me blind; I thought that only I had suffered at the hands of death."[7]

Perhaps no other grief is as blinding and debilitating as that over the loss of a child. In fact, research has shown that such a death can actually shorten the lives of affected parents.

A Danish study compared the health records of more than twenty-one thousand parents who had a child who'd died between 1980 and 1996 with nearly three hundred thousand parents whose children were still alive.[8]

Researchers found that women who had lost a child were much more likely to commit suicide or die in an accident or from disease compared with other mothers.

Fathers were twice as likely to commit suicide or die in an accident in the four years after the child's death, compared with other men. Doctors believe the grief and stress associated with such an event are to blame for the parents' increased rate of mortality.

Grief can register in a number of ways—as extreme stress, unremitting depression or melancholy, even anger and hostility. The grief-stricken may stop taking their medications and exercising; they may resume cigarette smoking, drinking, or abusing drugs to ease their suffering.

In the atmosphere of grief, the body is flooded with a sudden outpouring of stress hormones from the sympathetic nervous system, which increase heart rate and constrict arteries.

In fact, there is a medical condition called stress cardiomyopathy or "broken heart syndrome" that is often seen by emergency-room physicians in patients who are generally healthy and without a history of heart disease. Caused by intense emotional stress brought on by a sudden event, such as the shock of a loved one's death, the condition has all the symptoms of a heart attack—chest pain, shortness of breath, and heart muscle weakness.

Heart attacks happen when circulation to the heart muscle is cut off by a blood clot. In patients with coronary disease, emotional stress can precipitate a heart attack. But with broken heart syndrome, there are no blood clots or diseased arteries, only a unique ECG pattern, a mild cardiac enzyme elevation, and temporary weakening of the heart muscle's ability to pump.

Also called stress-induced heart failure, the condition seems to be caused by high levels of hormones that the body produces during severe stress, which can be temporarily toxic to the heart. One researcher found that levels of one hormone, catecholamine, or adrenaline, were thirty times higher than normal in those suffering from broken heart syndrome and up to five times the level seen in someone who's suffered a heart attack.[9]

Grief can cause such physiological changes while psychological processes are also occurring. Elisabeth Kübler-Ross's research highlighted the predictable stages that most people confront when facing their own deaths or the deaths of others. These stages include denial, anger, bargaining, depression, and finally acceptance. While not all people travel through each of these stages, most go through at least two of them.[10]

In healthy grieving, a kind of adaptation takes place over time as a person moves through these phases. It's not that a person completely loses the pain or sense of loss but that he eventually regains a sense of equilibrium. A person who doesn't pass through the various stages, however, may become mired in a particular stage, as Ken was stuck in denial.

The Indian monk Swami Vivekananda once wrote:

> Looking around us, what do we find? A continuous change. The plant comes out of the seed, grows into the tree, completes the circle, and comes back to the seed. The animal comes, lives a certain time, dies and completes the circle. So does man. The mountains slowly but surely crumble away, the rivers slowly but surely dry up, rains come out of the sea, and go back to the sea. Everywhere circles are being completed, birth, growth, development and decay following each other with mathematical precision. This is our everyday experience.[11]

The death of a child, however, isn't an everyday experience. The normal cycles of growth and development are interrupted. Such a death subverts the natural order. I knew this well, not only from my experience as a physician but also as a daughter and sister. Show me a parent who's lost a child and I'll show you one with a broken heart. My own father, Joseph, fell victim to such a tragedy. My father was an insurance man by day, a poet and comedian after hours. He was the one who insisted, in spite of the odds, that I'd be a doctor one day. None of us even *knew* a woman doctor in Bensonhurst, but that didn't keep my father from cherishing the belief that I'd be first.

Growing up, I didn't plan to be a physician but an anthropologist. I followed around my cousin's boyfriend, who was studying anthropology at Penn State, convincing myself that I wanted to be like him.

But another part of me yearned toward the living body rather than toward ancient artifacts, and my father realized it. He admired the calculus and biology homework I did at the dining-room table; he watched at the window when I went outside with a first-aid kit to help old Mr. Bartholemew when he fell off the curb and cut his hand.

"I'm telling you, Mimi, you're going to be a doctor."

"A doctor of *anthropology*," I said.

There was something Shakespearean and larger than life about my dad. He was a heavy drinker and a big laugher; when he sat at the table, all eyes gravitated to him. His side of the family was tough and prosperous; they carried themselves with a certain air of superiority. But none of that helped when tragedy struck our household a second time.

We were all still reeling from the early death of my mother when my older brother died in a drowning accident at the age of fifteen. This second punch was the one that knocked out my father. Though this death was traumatic for all of us, my father took it especially hard.

He'd already had a cardiac condition, but it worsened after my brother's death. Yet he was stoic and never said a word about how he felt. He remained mired in the depression stage of grief, losing the will to live himself and dying at the age of fifty from coronary disease. Had he been able to move past his grief or turn it into action, as members of groups such as Mothers Against Drunk Driving do, the end result might have been different.

I might have recognized Ken's tight chest and false smile, since it was so similar to my father's. But I hadn't allowed myself. After all, this was a grief I'd harboured, too.

In Ken's case, after visits to therapists, clergy, and other physicians, an unusual opportunity presented itself. A friend, aware of Ken and Cindy's inconsolable grief, offered them an appointment with a well-known psychic, a deeply religious man who claimed that he had the ability to communicate with departed souls. Although skeptical, by then Ken and his wife were so desperate that they agreed to keep the appointment.

They drove several hours to a nearby town, where the psychic lived in a nondescript ranch house in the midst of a small suburban neighborhood. The psychic, Henry, was an average looking, sand-haired man who was modest about his talents.

"My powers are simply a gift I've been given. I don't take any credit for them," he said after he greeted them. "I just hope I can help."

The psychic knew only one fact: that the couple had lost a child. After sitting down with them in his office, he talked about the concept of the afterlife he believed in—a place in which physical pain and mental anguish are gone.

Then he closed his eyes and seemed to sink into a deep concentration. "I'm picking up the image of a young boy who has passed on. He has brown hair cut in a Buster Brown haircut. I see him as a happy-go-lucky child with many friends."

Ken was not overly impressed by this preliminary information, thinking that the psychic had a fifty-fifty chance of guessing a boy and that the rest of it was suitably vague.

But Cindy was shaken. "That's George!" she said, taking Ken's arm.

The psychic continued: "I'm picking up a bird now, a big one, in shades of blue. Does this make any sense?"

"No," Ken said gruffly.

"I'm definitely seeing it," the psychic said. "I think it may be an eagle."

Ken shook his head.

"I'm seeing it in a private spot, a place that never sees the sun."

All at once Cindy began weeping. "The tattoo!" she cried.

The night before his death, one of George's friends had given him a tattoo kit and had stenciled an ink tattoo of an eagle on the boy's lower back. George had been so taken with it that he had stood in the mirror admiring it all evening and refused to take a bath, lest it wash off.

That the psychic had picked this up astounded even Ken; it was a fact that no one except they themselves and George's friend could possibly have known. The couple were further thunderstruck by the accuracy of the private family information the psychic continued to provide:

their deceased dog's breed; the location of their honeymoon vacation; the nickname they had called their son.

Finally, Henry said, "If you feel comfortable with what I've just told you, I have a message from your son."

Cindy nodded and looked to Ken, who was showing signs of intense distress. He had begun to sweat, and his hands were shaking. He buried his face in his hands. "I don't know!"

"I won't do anything you're uncomfortable with ..."

"Ken, please," Cindy said. "We might not have another chance."

Ken uncovered his face and looked at his wife's beseeching face. "All right. Go ahead."

"Okay," Henry said. "This is especially for you, Ken. George wants you to know that even though he was only a boy, his purpose in life was over, and it was his time to pass. He's come to accept this, and he wants you to accept it, too. And there's another thing—he wants you to continue with the talking books. He says that M is waiting—does that make any sense?"

"George!" Ken cried out. The dam in him finally had broken, and all the emotions he'd walled off since his son's death seemed to rush out. He buried his head in his hands again and wept like a baby.

Henry slipped out of the room and left the couple alone. When Ken pulled himself together, he told Henry just how amazingly accurate the message had been.

Ken's publishing company had long sponsored a volunteer program that distributed audiobooks to the ill and destitute at hospitals and shelters. George had liked to accompany his father on these junkets, especially to the local children's hospital, where he had met a boy named Mark, around his age, who was suffering from cancer. Both boys enjoyed the Harry Potter series, and Mark had been looking forward to the next book, which had come out after George's death. But Ken had not been able to bring himself to continue with this work or visit the hospital again.

Though a religious man, Ken had never expected the kind of relief this visit provided him. In the weeks that followed, he found that he was able to talk to his wife, look at photos of George, help clean out the boy's room . . . in effect, to make some sort of peace with his boy's passing. And, perhaps most therapeutic, he was able to return to the volunteer work that had apparently meant so much.

It wasn't that Ken's heart problems were totally eradicated by this development; they weren't. But what broke down in Ken also broke him open. He began seeing a grief counselor; he wasn't so compulsive about exercising. The stress reduction that he did finally penetrated the bedrock of who he was.

Experts say that it's essential for the grief-stricken to find a way to channel their pain. Doing so can change lives in extraordinary ways. This was the case with Linda and Peter Biehl when they were confronted with the almost unbearable death of their daughter Amy.

An idealistic white college student, Amy Biehl travelled to South Africa after winning a Fulbright scholarship in order to assist the anti-apartheid movement. While there, she was caught in a race riot and murdered by a black mob.

After years of grief, Amy's parents gave up their upper-middle- class life and moved from California to South Africa. They established a foundation in their daughter's name and attempted to complete the work she had started. In the process, they met two of the young men responsible for their daughter's death. Upon learning of the chaotic circumstances of the riot and the killers' remorse, the Biehls eventually even befriended them. The young men asked to atone for their crime by doing public service for the foundation the Biehls had established. For two years they worked with Amy's parents daily. Eventually they became so close that they addressed Linda Biehl as "Mom." Both of the elder Biehls reported that they felt more at peace after forgiving their daughter's killers.[12]

The minister and author Wayne Muller writes about how those of us who believe we'll live a long time become sloppy and live heedlessly, squandering our time. But the death of a loved one can make us suddenly and acutely aware of how death frames all our existences, and how precious life is.

Being brought face-to-face with the brevity of our existence makes us question our place in the scheme of things; it opens us up to explorations of the meaning of fulfillment and destiny.

In examining what galvanizes our passion and curiosity, Muller writes: "Curiosity, of course, shares the same root as 'cure,' so in a way what we love and what captures our curiosity draws us forward into some place of great destiny." [13]

I have been challenged and sustained by two questions Wayne Muller has posed in his writings: What kind of people shall we be, knowing that we have only a short period left here on this earth? How shall we live, knowing that we will die?

Whenever people ask why I chose to specialize in cardiology, I tell them that with the heart, there are ways you can help. There are procedures such as stents and bypass that can actually turn a person's life around and provide him or her with years of productive life. What could be more satisfying than opening an artery, allowing a fresh flow of lifeblood into a patient's starving heart?

This was a true but easy answer, perfect for public consumption, but I knew it was more than that.

The cath lab I worked in was located thousands of miles from my roots, but I still had New York all over me. I'd not only incorporated into my being my old-fashioned childhood but all the people I'd loved and lost, as well as their various dreams, which had been grafted onto me like a tree.

It would have been a heady experience for any physician to treat scores of patients, to see them arrive weak and frail one day and walk out, restored, the next. But for me it felt like a karmic act, some divine retribution for my family's deaths.

How many lives would need to be saved before I felt that something in the universe had been corrected, that my early loss had been avenged? For that, there is no easy answer. Perhaps I haven't reached it yet.

Part III
Beyond the Physical Heart

Chapter Eight

The Little Brain

If I asked, "Where do you feel love?" you probably wouldn't place your hand on your neck or stomach, but over the upper left side of your chest—the region of your heart. And if I asked you to describe the feeling, you might describe a sensation of pleasant fullness or swollen gladness. This is how love *feels*.

But how do you know this?

Western science has long believed that the brain is the bearer of these tidings—the ruler of the vast communication network of our body. In this view, the brain responds to external stimuli and causes emotions over which we have only slight control. When we confront a loved one, a fearful image, or a dangerous situation, the brain alone was once perceived as the courier, rushing messages to the rest of our body, which waited passively for instruction.

Research by John and Beatrice Lacey in the 1960s and 1970s, however, demonstrated that this model was not entirely accurate. The heart, the Laceys discovered, was not just a pump but also an organ of great intelligence, with its own nervous system, decision-making powers, and connections to the brain. They found that the heart actually "talks" with the brain, communicating with it in ways that affect how we perceive and react to the world.

Over two decades of research, the Laceys also found that the heart had its own unique logic, which often diverged from the command of the autonomic nervous system. They theo-rized that the heart "tuned" the senses and indirectly the muscles with a language that is transformed into nerve impulses that permeate the brain.[1]

In 1991, Dr. J. Andrew Armour introduced the concept of a functioning "heart brain." His book *Neurocardiology*, coedited with Dr. Jeffrey L. Ardell, focussed on the heart's intrinsic nervous system, composed of a complex network of neurons and neurotransmitters. The elaborate circuitry of this "little brain" allows it to act independently of the cranial brain—to learn, remember, even sense and feel.

Armour's pioneering work in neurocardiology demonstrated that each beat of the heart sends complex signals to the brain and other organs. These heart signals are capable of reaching higher brain centers, ultimately affecting our reasons and choices, our emotions and perceptions. Apparently, the heart has not only its own language but its own *mind*.

In 1983, the heart was reclassified as an endocrine gland when it was discovered to produce a hormone called atrial natriuretic factor, or ANF. This is yet another way that the heart communicates with the brain and other organs—through the production of hormones and neurotransmitters, such as dopamine and adrenaline, which are known to mediate emotion.

These scientific advances illuminate the fact that while we may believe the brain is our decision maker and ruler, the tenounce heart is more powerful than we ever imagined—functioning as a sensory organ, hormone-producing gland, and information-processing center.[2]

The debate over the centrality of the heart versus the brain is an ancient one. Which of these organs was the seat of the soul and the mastermind of thought and behavior was once the cause of such a heated argument that there were two different camps. Those who believed in the heart's primacy were termed cardiocentrists and those who believed in the brain cerebrocentrists.

Ancient Egyptians were cardiocentrists who believed the heart was associated with the soul. During ritual embalming, the heart was treated with great reverence, while the brain was considered relatively worthless. In fact, Egyptian kings were mummified for the next life with everything *but* the brain, which was scooped out or removed through the nose. A passage from *The Book of the Dead*, which gives advice and aid on reaching the underworld, reads, "O my heart which I had from my mother . . . Hail to you, my heart, hail to you my entrails!"[3]

Ancient Indian medicine also paid special reverence to the heart, as did traditional Chinese medicine, which believed the heart governed the blood vessels and stored spirit. And Hazrat Inayat Khan, a sage of Sufism who spoke of the "religion of the heart," wrote: "The body is the instrument of the mind. . . . The mind is an instrument of the heart."[4]

In ancient Greece, Aristotle believed that since the heart was "central, mobile, and hot, and well supplied with structures which served to communicate between it and the rest of the body," it was most suitable to be the seat of the soul.[5]

But Plato viewed the body as a guardhouse and the head as the citadel. He saw the heart as simply a "knot of veins and the fountain of the blood,"[6] and the head the governing part of the body.

No matter which view is taken, the heart possesses special attributes that give it su-premacy over the brain as the key organ for our survival. It is formed first and stops last. By the sixth week of pregnancy, when the foetus is no bigger than a marble, the cardiac muscle has already formed and begun its initial fluttering movements. Life can continue without the brain, but not once the heart has stopped.

The electromagnetic current of the heart is sixty times higher in amplitude than the field of the brain. It also emits an energy field five thousand times stronger than the brain's, one that can be measured more than ten feet from the body.

The heart is also exquisitely sensitive to emotions. An angry or fearful thought changes the heart-rate variability (HRV) pattern—the beat-to-beat variability between each heartbeat—which sets the pace for the brain and the respiratory system.

It's long been known that emotions have a physiological impact on our bodies. Plato saw emotions as wild horses that required restraint by the intellect, while in Christian theology, emotions were viewed as sins that must be resisted by the use of reason.[7]

But what if it's not the brain telling the heart what to feel, but the heart informing the rest of the body? What if changing the mind actually involves changing the heart?

Marta Jennings was a successful lawyer in her mid-fifties—slender, ambitious, driven, and tightly wound. She dressed in tight bright suits and wore her hair in a sleek, short bob. She gave the impression of great impatience, as if something around the corner was always pending and far more important than the business at hand. Some part of her was constantly in motion; if she had to wait, even for a moment, she tapped her fingers or rattled the gold jew-elry on her long arms.

Regal in her manner, she was accustomed to working hard and having her way. A power walker, red wine drinker, and careful eater, she had the taut, toned look of healthy prosperity. Regularly weighed, scanned, and tested, she was proud of her high HDL and low LDL levels and considered herself in perfect health.

When I met her, she and her husband were in the process of moving to an exclusive California beach community where they had purchased a house that they wanted to convert to a retirement mansion. Marta had every detail planned and a tight deadline for completion, from the plush carpet to the pickled oak flooring to the imported marble for the baths.

But the local zoning board had thrown a wrench into her plans by requiring her to appear before a review board before beginning these extensive renovations. She had tried pulling strings in order to bypass this request, but there was no way to circumvent it. She had used her considerable funds to hire a top-notch architectural team, who had drawn up elaborate plans.

Her months of effort now rested on her presentation to the board for approval. When the day finally arrived for her to make her case, she brought along not only her plans but also the architect who had drawn them up, certain that her appearance was only a formality.

But from the moment she arrived at the meeting, events did not proceed as she had planned. She was placed at the end of the roster and had to cool her heels while listening to a roomful of other applicants. Once again, in spite of her wealth and status, there was nothing she could do about this. For a personality such as Marta's, being stymied or feeling out of control was almost unbearable and produced teeth-clenching frustration. As she listened to other people's garage plans, landscape designs, and arguments over surveys, she grew more exasperated and furious.

When she was called to the podium to present her case, she was livid. But even worse, as she presented her case, it became clear that the board was not just unsympathetic but actually hostile to her. Her extensive and expensive architect didn't work in her favour but against it.

She was told that her renovation was at odds with local ordinances, that the size of her expansion plans exceeded zoning requirements, and that she would have to resubmit a more modest design plan at the next meeting, later in the year.

Marta was beside herself. "That's impossible! I object!" she stated, but the chairman said, "Next," and moved on.

By the time she stormed out of the session, Marta was so furious that her chest was tight and she was having difficulty breathing.

When she arrived home and told her husband what had happened, he didn't share her outrage. "So we'll do it later," he said. "What's the big deal?"

"What's the big deal? Are you serious?" And there in her carpeted bedroom, as Marta paced and fumed, her adrenal glands began releasing cortisol, elevating her blood sugar and infusing her body with extra energy; the release of epinephrine increased her heart rate and blood pressure. She began to overbreathe or hyperventilate. Internally, she was triggering a whole cascade of physiological processes as severe as if she were face-to-face with a legitimately catastrophic event.

In fact, had her heart been monitored during those moments, her heart-rate variability would have appeared as chaotic and erratic as her behavior.

Her husband, Harold, called an ambulance. When the paramedics arrived, they quickly assessed Marta's heart rate and blood pressure, and they placed electrodes on her chest for an electrocardiogram. The jagged line of the ECG appeared on a portable monitor, and the image was transmitted to the hospital emergency room.

When Marta arrived at the hospital, the physician performed a physical examination and a more complete ECG as well as blood tests.

Then he walked into her cubicle, where she was propped up, still in full makeup and jewelry, and said, "Mrs. Jennings, I'm afraid you've suffered a mild heart attack."

"A *what*?" her husband whispered.

Even though Marta was hooked up to a heart monitor, she still managed to cause a commotion.

"That's ridiculous! I couldn't have had a heart attack. I had a heart scan a month ago, and I had no calcification or blockages whatsoever! I want to speak to my own doctor."

The nurses managed to calm her down, but Marta insisted that her physician be called, and he was eventually reached by phone.

After conferring with the ER physician and having a coronary angiogram performed, her doctor told Marta that while it was true that she had normal coronary arteries without blockages, the damage to her heart muscle had been caused by a condition called vasospasm.

A temporary, abrupt contraction of the muscles in the wall of a coronary artery, vaso-spasm slows or stops blood flow to the heart. The condition, like broken heart syndrome, is more prevalent in women than in men. Officially, Marta's condition was termed "severe coronary spasm in the setting of stress."

"What could have caused something like this?" her husband asked.

"What were you doing beforehand?" the doctor asked.

"I was at a meeting," she said.

"What kind of meeting?"

"It was nothing—just a review board."

"Marta . . ." her husband said.

"Okay," she snapped. "It was a stressful situation, but that's nothing out of the ordinary for me."

"Well, there you are," the doctor said.

But Marta wasn't ready to accept that her heart attack could have been the direct result of stress and emotions and the physiological reactions that they had created in her body.

Nor was she able to accept a notion that she considered even more outrageous—that it was actually within her power to have prevented it.

It has long been recognized that stress affects the cardiovascular system, a result of the release of stress hormones. But in some people, the rush of adrenaline can be especially toxic.

Almost a century ago, a Harvard Medical School physiologist, Walter Cannon, showed that changes in emotion are accompanied by predictable alterations in heart rate, respiration, blood pressure, and digestion through the influence of the autonomic nervous sys-tem. Cannon published a now-famous essay on "Voodoo Death." Drawing on accounts from anthropologists, Cannon verified that people who were flooded with fear, resulting from the belief that they had been hexed by voodoo, curses, or magical incantations, could actually fall ill and die from a sudden and massive stress response.[8]

One particular case involved the taboo system of the Maori aborigines of New Zealand. Cannon told of a young aborigine who stopped off at the home of an older friend while travelling. For breakfast, the friend prepared a meal consisting of wild hen, a food strictly forbidden by tradition and custom. The young man demanded to know if there was wild hen in the meal, and his host said no. At this reassurance, he ate the forbidden food in ignorance and later departed.

Several years later, the two met again and the older friend asked the younger if he would now eat wild hen. The boy said he never would because it was taboo. The older man laughed and told him how he had tricked him into eating this forbidden food long ago. The young man began to tremble and became extremely frightened; within twenty-four hours, he was dead. No disease or virus, simply his emotional fear and stress.

More recent research[9] has shown that men who complain of high anxiety are up to six times more likely than calmer men to suffer sudden cardiac death. A twenty-year study by researchers at the University of London concluded that unmanaged reactions to stress were a more dangerous risk factor for heart disease and cancer than either smoking or high choles-terol.[10] And a Harvard Medical School Study of 1,122 heart attack survivors found that those who tried to remain calm during emotional conflict had half the risk of heart attacks compared with those who tended to get angry.[11]

The challenge is how to translate this knowledge in a way that can help people in the present instead of filling medical journals that are read only by physicians.

Researchers at the Institute of HeartMath seem to have found a way.

"The heart has a mind that some might call the spirit, the higher self, intuition or the small voice within. How many times have you said to yourself, 'If only I had listened to my heart.' By not listening, we often pay a price in time and energy in cleaning up the mess afterward." This according to Rolin McCraty, head researcher at the Institute of HeartMath, a nonprofit research and education organization that has built upon the work of the Laceys, studying the physiological mechanisms by which the heart communicates with the brain.

Over the years, HeartMath has conducted research validating the power of the heart in relieving stress and promoting health. They've formulated practical interventions that incorporate the understanding that the heart profoundly affects our perceptions, awareness, and intelligence. I wanted Marta to utilize one of the HeartMath techniques that teaches how to shift powerfully negative emotion to positive ones.

When I met with Marta in my office a few days after her hospitalization, she was still furious because her illness was conflicting with her social plans, including a trip to Hawaii.

When I walked in, she was on her cell phone talking to her travel agent. "I don't care—I expect a total refund! I don't know when we can reschedule—here's my new doctor, hopefully she can give me more information."

She clicked off and bombarded me with questions: What was her prognosis, what were her restrictions, what reassurances could I give her that this kind of incident would never inconvenience her again?

"I can't answer those questions. These issues are up to you."

"What do you mean? Can't you just give me some medicine . . . what about the beta-blockers and statins my husband is taking?"

"Certainly I can start you on medication, but you must address the underlying cause of your heart disease. After reviewing your records, I think you're going to have to do some work controlling your stress and emotions."

"Well, I'm not about to swallow my feelings! I've got a right to my anger!"

She cherished the commonly held belief that it is actually healthy to vent anger and other hostile emotions. But emotionally stressful events, and more specifically anger, precede and may even trigger the onset of a heart attack. In one study, episodes of anger were found to be capable of triggering a heart attack in the two hours after the outburst.[12]

For Marta, defensiveness and anger were her default positions—the stances she lapsed into automatically throughout the day. She seemed to savour, even to be proud of, the part of her personality that was chronically demanding and aggressive. In fact, she actually wanted to postpone working on any of these cardiac issues until one of several litigations she was involved in was settled.

"I'll try and calm down until this next case is over," she said, flipping through her appointment book. "I think I can schedule it in three weeks, maybe after the twelfth."

"Marta, I'm going to show you something. And I really want you to pay attention."

She looked up at me from over her half-glasses as I handed her a page of lab reports.

"These are the cardiac blood enzyme reports from when you entered the hospital."

"Okay."

"Here are your levels; here's the normal range."

She studied the numbers.

"It doesn't matter that you have no blockages or diseased arteries on your angiogram. It doesn't matter that your heart scan shows no calcifications. It doesn't matter that you're slender and have no risk factors for coronary disease. You have had a heart attack all the same. This isn't some minor inconvenience you can handle with a quick procedure. And you have a good deal of control about what happens to you from now on."

"What are you saying?"

"I'm saying that the spasm of your coronary artery was most likely caused by intense stress combined with your emotional outburst. If you had been able to shift your thinking and better control your emotions, I don't think you would have had a heart attack in the first place. I'm saying it's in your power to defuse the emotions that nearly killed you."

Finally, she shut her appointment book, put down her pen, and took off her glasses. My words seemed to have penetrated her tough shell. She actually looked close to tears.

Marta was faced with a situation that neither her status nor her money could solve. She had to face the fact that her healing was now up to her.

Larry Dossey writes, "Scientists working in the new field of psychoneuroimmunology have demonstrated the existence of infinite links between parts of the brain concerned with thought and emotion and the neurological and immune systems. Based on these discoveries, we know beyond doubt that thought can become biology." [13]

Viewed through the lens of this new science, Marta's anger, frustration, and rage were not simply emotions but potent physiological states that could affect her health as much as high cholesterol.

Far from being regular, the rhythms of the heart can vary drastically from moment to moment. In fact, these rhythms are the most dynamic and reflective of our states of inner stress and emotion.

By measuring heart-rate variability, researchers have been able to analyse how the heart and nervous system respond to stress and emotions. Negative emotions such as rage and frustration lead to increased disorder in the autonomic nervous system and in the heart's rhythm—a chaotic HRV pattern adversely affects the whole body. But positive feelings, such as appreciation and love, produce heart-rhythm coherence, inner harmony, and increased health. Since the heart is the most powerful oscillator in the body, the rhythm set by the heart is capable of entraining other organs to oscillate in synchronicity.

It's possible to view what venting negative emotions such as Marta's look like as opposed to feelings of love and appreciation. In the midst of rage, heart-rate variability patterns are chaotic. But the pattern shifts to a coherent and orderly one when a person enters a loving, appreciative state.

Emotional stakes also alter the levels of immunoglobulin A (IgA), a key player in the body's immunological defense system. This was vividly illustrated in a Harvard study that found an upswing in IgA among subjects who watched a compassion inducing videotape featuring Mother Teresa.[14] A HeartMath study comparing the effects of anger versus compassion on the immune system found that a single five-minute period during which a person emotionally and mentally recalls an angry episode inhibited the production of IgA, suppress-ing the immune system for more than six hours.[15] On the other hand, self-induced feelings of compassion increased the production of IgA, significantly enhancing the immune system.[16] As a cardiologist, I know that low heart-rate variability can be as important as cholesterol levels. I wanted Marta to utilize a core HeartMath technique called Freeze Frame—in which patients freeze a stressful situation, as if it were a frame in a movie, then consciously shift to a positive emotion in order to reverse the effects of hostility and stress. People who practice this emotional self-management technique are able to generate consistent changes in their electrocardiogram output when requested to radiate love, appreciation, compassion, or other positive emotions.

That day, at our appointment, I said to Marta, "I'd like to ask you a personal question."

"Go ahead."

"Who or what do you love the most?"

This simple question seemed to stump and annoy her, and she responded in her typical irritable fashion.

"What's that got to do with anything? I'm not into this touchy-feely stuff."

"Think about it for a few minutes and I'll be right back."

When I returned a little while later, I found her sorting through bits of paper from her billfold.

"Here," she said gruffly, holding out a wallet size photo of a young girl with long ringlets, dressed in a pink princess dress and a tinfoil crown. "That's my answer."

"Who's this?"

"My granddaughter."

"I didn't know you had a granddaughter."

"I never mention it. I ... Well, I just don't see her very often."

"What's her name?"

"Mia." She looked at the photo again. "And now I've gotten myself furious just thinking about how little involvement I have in her life."

"Good, you're angry . . . we've got the perfect environment to try this. Come with me."

We walked down the hall to one of our computers. "I'm going to hook you up."

"Great . . . another expensive test."

I placed Marta's finger into a fingertip pulse sensor, linked to a computer that contained HeartMath software.

"Now let's see what this anger of yours looks like. Concentrate a moment more on your resentment and negative feelings."

"That's easy," Marta said. She exhaled and a jagged line appeared on the computer screen.

"Just the way I feel," she said.

"Now I want you to stop this reaction and shift your attention to your heart. Concentrate on your heart."

"Okay."

"Now hold it there for at least ten seconds while you think of Mia."

Marta sat up straighter and breathed in deeply. "Okay, I'm doing it."

"Now I want you to generate a sincere positive feeling of caring and appreciation."

Her line on the screen remained jagged.

Marta frowned. "I'm not sure what you want."

"Keep your focus on your heart. Think of Mia and concentrate on your love and gratitude for her."

"Okay, I'm trying."

"Don't think of it as a test or a chore. Relax, Marta. Open your heart and feel your love."

At that, some internal shift seemed to occur in her. We watched together as the line gradually straightened and eventually became a smooth, coherent wave.

"Look at that!" Marta said.

The cardiologist Harvey Zarren used a version of this technique with his patients when he rode in the ambulance with them en route to the hospital. During these harrowing rides, he asked them to discuss the thing in life that they loved most, and their heart rate and blood pressure fell miraculously. According to Zarren, none of his patients ever had a cardiac arrest in the ambulance when they did this.[17]

Other research has shown that simply looking at a photograph of a loved one can help dampen stress and that thinking about supportive friends for a few moments before a stressful test minimizes increases in heart rate and blood pressure.[18]

After a few moments, I asked Marta: "How do you feel?"

She looked at me. "Calm. Better. My heart was pounding before, and now it's settled down a little."

She looked better, too; the slash down the center of her forehead had softened, and the perpetual grimace of her mouth had diminished.

"What this shows is that in a split second you can shift your autonomic nervous system from a sympathetic or stimulating state to a parasympathetic or relaxing one. When your heart rate is coherent like this, all kinds of beneficial changes are happening inside you."

"I can tell."

"You should practice this consistently—beginning with five Freeze Frames a day—in order to become accustomed to shifting from the head to the heart."

"That's it?" she asked.

"It's simple in some ways, but in others it's not. You're retraining a whole lifetime of reactions. And sincerity is a large component. You have to mean it—your heart knows when you're faking. You have to be sincere and do it regularly for there to be a continuing impact."

"Five times a day. That's not too bad," Marta said.

"You have to *mean* it," I stressed.

As the months passed, Marta began to see that she had used rage and anger to get her way since she was a child. She reacted with hostility and fury as unthinkingly as she turned the key in her car and drove to work. Such reactions become more than habitual; science now suggests that that they may actually become hardwired in the neural pathways of the brain. The more Marta entertained the same anxious, angry thoughts, the more likely it was for her body to return to the well-worn path and respond with damaging and stressful reactions. These recurring stress patterns are difficult to break using the mind alone; that's why HeartMath techniques, which focus on the power of the heart rather than on the power of the brain alone, are frequently successful.

As the author Aaron Antonovsky writes, "We've come to understand health not as the absence of disease but rather as the process by which individuals maintain their sense of coherence—their sense that life is comprehensible, manageable and meaningful—and ability to function in the face of changes in themselves and their relationships with their environment."[19]

A key finding of HeartMath research is that as people learn to sustain heart-focused positive states of feeling, the brain is brought into "entrainment" with the heart. In Marta's case, inducing coherence in her heart's rhythms also produced a shift in her perception and clarity of mind. Aligning herself with what she really loved—her granddaughter and family—allowed her to find resonance not only in her heartbeat but in her life.

There was another factor in Marta's cardiovascular disease and her unwillingness to accept the severity of her condition, one that impacts treatment and diagnosis for millions of people: the fact that she was a woman.

My patient Laurie was an anxious thirty-eight-year-old actress, the type of person who back in my neighbourhood would have been called a nervous wreck. Blond, petite, and youthfullooking, she was often cast in ingenue parts.

Her emotionality and sensitivity had helped her acting career, enabling her to pick up on the nuances of a variety of characters, but it had taken a heavy toll on her health. Over the years she had suffered from a variety of symptoms, including persistent muscle tightness, stomach upset, fatigue, and increasingly and ominously, chest discomfort and shortness of breath.

When she mentioned these last two symptoms to her general physician, he scoffed at her concerns.

"It's not your heart, it's not your heart, it's not your heart," he chanted, noting her fine cholesterol level, her young age, and the lack of heart disease in her family.

She had to press repeatedly before he finally ordered a stress test. The stress test was normal, further solidifying his position that she was simply suffering from anxiety and stress.

But when Laurie began to suffer from these symptoms with increased regularity, she took her test results to two other physicians and received much the same reaction. She was assured by both that she had no cardiovascular disease and told by one that her symptoms were caused by costochondritis, an inflammation of connective tissue in the chest wall. She was prescribed medication to raise her mood and to help alleviate chest discomfort.

Why were both of these physicians so swift to discount Laurie's symptoms? Perhaps because she was not the stereotype of someone with heart disease—an overweight, middle-aged man.

Her chest pain and shortness of breath were enclosed in the wrapper of a young woman with long blond hair and a petite figure. Her doctors harbored the dangerous preconception that women, especially young women, are not likely to have heart disease. Laurie did not have the *look* of cardiovascular disease.

But the reality is staggeringly different. Women have gained equality in this area, if no other. Even though there are far more awareness, stigma, and terror about breast cancer, which kills approximately forty-three thousand women a year, five hundred thousand women die yearly from heart disease—a figure that exceeds the next seven causes of death com-bined.[20] And women are more likely to die following a heart attack than men.

In spite of this, women vastly downplay their risk of heart disease—only 35 percent in one study associated their symptoms with cardiovascular disease, often attributing them to another ailment.[21]

It's no wonder women don't recognize their risk; often their physicians don't either. In one study, five hundred physicians from around the country were asked to evaluate the records of male and female patients and make recommendations for treatment. Fewer than one in five doctors were aware that more women than men die of heart disease each year.[22]

In another study, the National Institute of Nursing Research found that women experience undiagnosed warning signs weeks, months and even years, before having a heart attack, as Laurie did.[23]

One reason why women's symptoms are often undertreated and undiagnosed is that they can be more ambiguous than men's crushing chest pain and left arm discomfort. The top five symptoms of women in one study were unusual fatigue, difficulty sleeping, shortness of breath, indigestion, and anxiety.[24]

Research has also shown that women are far less likely than men to receive basic medical care that could significantly reduce their heart attack and stroke risk. Many physi-cians order fewer tests for women and prescribe fewer preventive measures, such as daily aspirin, diet, and cholesterol- and blood-pressure-lowering medications.[25]

A Michigan study based on records of 1,511 people who had sustained heart attacks found that women wait significantly longer than men to receive emergency angioplasty, which can reopen blocked blood vessels and restore blood flow to the heart muscle. This intervention has the largest impact if it is performed within ninety minutes of a patient's arrival in an emergency room; the longer a patient waits for this treatment, the higher the chances of permanent heart damage. Yet women waited more than 118 minutes for treatment, compared with a man's 105. This delay, added to the extra 20 minutes it takes for the typical woman to reach the emergency room after her symptoms start, results in a half hour more of wasted time.[26]

It was remarkable how nearly all these factors played out in Laurie.

The week before our meeting, she had been audi-tioning for a part in a major theatrical production and had been under more than her usual amount of anxiety and stress.

Her shortness of breath grew increasingly worse, as did the dull ache in her chest. The night after her audition she also developed more classic symptoms, including pain in her left arm and chest pressure.

She called her sister, a nurse in a nearby city, and told her how she felt and that her recent stress test had been normal.

"I don't care what anyone else tells you. Go to the hospital *now*," her sister insisted.

When Laurie arrived at the emergency room, her heart rate, and blood pressure were quickly assessed and electrodes placed on her chest for an ECG. Even though the ECG showed changes suggestive of heart disease, she was released several hours later, diagnosed with gallstones.

By then, Laurie strongly felt that she'd been misdiagnosed and immediately made an appointment, bringing along copies of her latest records.

By the time we met, she had been evaluated by multiple physicians. Her condition had been variously called generalized anxiety, costochondritis, and gallbladder stones. Yet there were the signs of coronary disease, clear as day, on her ECG.

As for her much-touted stress test, her walking treadmill hadn't sufficiently raised her heart rate and blood pressure to assess adequately for coronary blockage. Furthermore, these standard stress tests have been found to be less reliable in women.[27] In Laurie's case, a nuclear stress test, which looks at blood flow to the heart muscle, might have provided more accurate results.

When I first asked her to tell me about the experiences that had brought her to my office, Laurie looked at me oddly.

"Are you sure you have time?" she asked warily. "It's kind of a long story."

"I have time."

"Do you want the abridged or the full version?"

"I want the real version," I said.

According to my office clock, Laurie talked for fourteen and a half minutes, almost nonstop—not that long when you consider she was telling me her whole life. She told me about being a child in the Midwest, about leaving home to go to college, about moving to the West Coast and finding work she loved. She talked about how her cascade of physical symptoms had increasingly made her feel frail and vulnerable.

Once Laurie began talking, she couldn't seem to stop. "I don't know why I'm telling you all this," she kept saying, but I knew why. It was the story of her heart.

She ended by talking about how she had felt intuitively, for some time, that she had problems with her heart. "They say you're supposed to pay attention to your body, but when I did, no one would listen."

"Your body was telling the truth," I said, when she finished. "I'm sorry it took so long for someone to hear you."

An angiogram was ultimately performed on Laurie, and I showed her the results.

"There's a blockage in the main artery called the LAD. This is what has been causing your symptoms. I would like to place a stent right here to unblock this artery."

I put my hand on her shoulder as Laurie studied the shadowy image of her own arterial map.

"I knew it," she whispered.

At a follow-up appointment, I asked, "Laurie, what's the most important thing a phy-sician could have done to make your whole ordeal this past year better?"

And she looked up at me and said, "You just did it, Dr. Guarneri. You took the time to listen."

Chapter Nine

Universal Heart

In the Far East, elephant trainers often secure a light tether—a simple length of rope—around a baby elephant's ankle to limit its range. As the baby grows, the trainers regularly reinforce the boundary of this rope. By the time the elephant is an adult, he has matured into a huge and powerful animal who has the strength to easily break this bond. But by then he has grown so accustomed to being restrained that he has no conception of the strength he possesses to free himself.

As humans, we are also conditioned to live within a limited perception of our own consciousness and power. We're taught by Western science to consider ourselves separate souls, bags of flesh containing glands and bones, "islands of consciousness confronting an alien world," as the philosopher Alan Watts puts it.[1] We are encouraged to believe that the mind, body, and spirit are split and fragmented, that if we can't quantify something, it's not real.

But what if we weren't really living in a world of division, separation, and alienation, but one of connection and interdependence?

What if we were all part of the same source and blueprint, woven together in an inherent unity that is infinite and enduring? What if we knew scientifically that everything in the universe is eternal, alive, and evolving?

What if consciousness isn't contained in the body, as the Western model claims, but the body is contained in consciousness?

This is what a convergence of ground breaking research combining quantum mechanics, cellular memory, and nonlocal mind suggests.

Viewed through the lens of this new science, the heart is revealed as an organ of consciousness and memory that orchestrates an intricate symphony of data and energy and may be the seat of our souls.

Quantum theory suggests that there is something nonlocal that connects matter across space and time, a belief explored by the author and health educator Dr. Larry Dossey.

In *Reinventing Medicine*,[2] Dossey identifies three periods through which medicine progressed in the second half of the nineteenth century—Eras I, II, and III. Era I, mechanical medicine, began around the 1860s and still dominates our system. The central belief of this period is that since both illness and health are completely physical in nature, so are their cures—from surgical procedures to medications. This era of medicine locates the mind or consciousness within the brain.

The period following World War II, Era II, saw the development of what we now call mind-body medicine. Physicians began to acknowledge that there was a psychosomatic aspect to illness and that stress and emotions could measurably influence health and disease.

The more recent Era III paradigm, which Dossey seeks to foster, proposes that consciousness is not confined to an individual body but can radiate outside it and impact others through such techniques as intercessory prayer, healing intention, and visualization. This era is characterized by "nonlocal mind"—mind spread infinitely throughout space and time, unconfined to the brain and body, eternal and immortal.

Nonlocality, according to Dossey, brings all of us together. In his view, "I am not separate from my patient or a boy I see walking on the beach or an old man dying in Bombay. They are at this very moment breathing air from the same universe as I am, living under the same dome of sky."

Dossey finds evidence for nonlocal mind in studies on the effects of distant healing and intercessory prayer. He found approximately 150 such studies, nearly half of which evidenced compelling statistical significance.[3] A number of them looked at the impact of distant intentionality on the healing rates of surgical wounds inflicted on rats or mice, while others considered its impact on the growth rates of yeast, fungi, and bacteria.

In a landmark study on humans, researchers studied healing intention, initiated at great distance, for patients who were ill with advanced AIDS.[4] The health of those patients who were the beneficiaries of these healing intentions was statistically better than those who did not receive it. Though the recipients were unaware that they were being prayed for, the healing intention still worked. Such research suggests that both prayer and positive intentions can be as profound when transmitted from the other side of the globe as at someone's side.

The psychoneuroimmunologist Dr. Paul Pearsall is another scientist and pioneer who has done ground breaking research on the transference of memories in organ transplant patients. After interviewing nearly 150 transplant recipients, Pearsall proposed the possibility of cellular memory—that the cells of living tissue have the capacity to remember and memorize characteristics of the human to whom they have belonged.

In Pearsall's view, the heart possesses its own unique intelligence, processing data about the body and the outside world.[5]

Pearsall writes, "It is generally assumed that learning involves primarily the nervous and secondarily the immune system. Hence patients receiving peripheral organ transplants should not experience personality changes that parallel those of donors they have never met."[6]

But evidence shows that some have. Twelve to fifteen percent of heart-transplant recipients report added characteristics following transplant of their new hearts.[7]

Although some of these changes may be attributed to medication and surgery, interesting anecdotes have evolved.

In his book *The Heart's Code*, Dr. Paul Pearsall describes interviews between heart transplant recipients and their donor families. There is the story of Glenda, a physician whose husband died in an auto accident. Still suffering from recurrent nightmares of the car lights that precipitated their head-on collision, Glenda requested to meet with the heart transplant recipient. Dr. Pearsall describes their meeting in a hospital chapel and Glenda's plea to place her hand on the young man's chest, hoping to feel her husband's heart. As Glenda sends her love to her husband, she tells him that everything is "copasetic." Surprised to hear this word, the young man's mother relates how her son began using this term immediately following his heart transplant. Amazed at this coincidence, she describes how her son, a former vegetarian, now loves meat and has replaced his love for heavy metal music with rock-and-roll oldies. Although Glenda immediately responds that her husband loved meat and played in a Motown band, one realizes the magnitude of this interaction when the heart transplant recipient reports having recurrent nightmares of a car's headlights heading towards him.

In my work as a cardiologist, I've witnessed many deaths and near deaths. In my field, more than others, people are often brought back to life after a cardiac arrest. I've had many experiences with patients who have told me that during the period when they were clinically dead, they felt infused with a sense of unity and peace.

This was the case with my patient Lisa, who was scheduled for a routine angioplasty. Overweight, depressed, in her late forties, she was a woman who seemed to have always existed under a cloud; her life had been one difficult struggle after another.

She was raising a young daughter alone after a bruising divorce; she'd developed rheumatoid arthritis and had recently lost her job with a local airline. Her coronary disease was only the most recent of a long line of misfortunes that seemed to follow her.

She was a particularly anxious patient and grasped my hand as she asked for reassurance that she'd be okay.

"This is a very safe procedure, Lisa," I told her, "but as with any cardiac procedure, I have to make you aware of the risks."

Even hearing about the small chance of complications made her frantic.

"You don't believe any of these will happen to me, do you?" She looked terrified.

"No, but I have to make you aware of them."

Perhaps Lisa had some presentiment of trouble, because in the midst of her procedure, she suffered an arrhythmia and her heart stopped beating.

This is one of those occurrences that you prepare for, but it is sobering to encounter nonetheless.

In most cases, it's possible to convert the heart back into a normal rhythm with a defibrillator, an electronic device with paddles and leads that delivers a shock, enabling the heart's natural pacemaker to regain control. But there are still those alarming seconds when the beat of life has stilled. Approximately 10 percent of the ability to restart the heart is lost with each minute that the heart remains in fibrillation. Unless the normal heart rhythm is restored, death can occur within minutes.

"Get the paddles!" I ordered, thinking instantly of Lisa's dark-haired daughter, whom I had glimpsed playing with a doll earlier in the waiting room.

The nurse positioned the crash cart—a cabinet containing the emergency equipment—and began setting up the defibrillator.

The paddles were placed on Lisa's chest and the nurse cried out, "Clear," a reminder for us to stand back, since touching Lisa while she was receiving a shock would cause us to be shocked as well.

After several jolts of electricity, I heard the reassuring staccato of Lisa's heartbeat, the most beautiful of sounds. I released all the air that I held trapped in my lungs, an exhalation of pure relief. For those moments, I'd seen Lisa's earthly life as a slender, shimmering thread, and I was grateful that it hadn't been broken.

But Lisa didn't see it that way.

We finished the procedure without further problems. Lisa remained in the hospital overnight, and she was released the next morning. I didn't see her for another week, when she came into my office, fuming.

"You know, I'm furious with you," she said after I examined her.

"I'm sorry you feel that way," I said, assuming she was upset about the complication during her procedure. "Arrhythmias sometimes occur because of the contrast injection, but usually the outcome is as successful as yours."

"No, I mean I didn't want you to bring me back. My life's so full of pain and problems. The place I was at when my heart stopped was full of light and peace. There were all these people I'd lost—my grandmother and my father."

"I'd say I'm sorry, but I'm not," I told her. "I'm very relieved that we were able to get your heart beating again."

Lisa looked out the window. "I know. It's just that for a while, I wasn't worried. I wasn't in pain. I finally felt like I belonged.. . ."

My encounter with Lisa occurred early in my career as a cardiologist, before I realized that what she had experienced during those moments wasn't an aberration but a glimpse of a truth that we, like the tethered elephants, have been perceptually restrained from seeing.

It is the same startling realization that research on cellular memory and nonlocal mind leads to—that we are not separate, alienated bits of consciousness but part of a unified and eternal whole.

When I was younger, I concentrated solely on the life force of each individual. Whenever there was a death, I felt it as a singular, painful tear in the universe, an unacceptable and grievous loss. After I lost my parents, I used to think forlornly that I could search the most remote parts of the earth and there would be no trace of them—so precious and irreplaceable were they.

But once I became a doctor, I began to change my perspective. I began to perceive the force that flows through all of us, that unites Paul and Russ, Marta and Lisa, my grandmother and brother, into a single fabric that is the structure of existence itself.

I came to appreciate the collective heart in all its infinite variety—starting its timid tick deep in a mother's womb just as an ancient heart in a nursing home finally falls silent, so that the beat continues throughout time—the rhythm of our great, eternal life.

Chapter Ten

Toward Compassionate Medicine

My path as a physician was influenced by my uncle, an old-fashioned general practitioner on Long Island. His waiting room was always crammed with patients, a cross section of the neighbourhood, the elderly jammed in with mothers holding wailing babies in their arms.

"Why does everyone want to see him?" I asked my aunt, who served as his office assistant.

"Because he takes his time and pays attention to what they say."

I knew what was in my uncle's office because I was allowed to wander around it after hours, and it was laughably rudimentary compared with our technological offices now: gauze, alcohol, Mercurochrome, swabs, stethoscope and antibiotics.

There were no cures for blocked arteries or narrowed heart valves back then. But you would have never known that from the look of relief on the faces of my uncle's patients when they left his examining room.

Compassion, patience, empathy—these were the tools doctors like my uncle used until medicine changed, when powerful economic forces began to influence the length and scope of a patient's visit.

Patients expected physicians to use their expertise *and* their humanity to take in the often complicated accounts of their bodies and lives and interpret them into some kind of diagnosis. They expected doctors to discern, to read their symptoms and place them in a meaningful context, to be an interpreter of their maladies.

And patients still expect and yearn for their doctors to do this.

When I was growing up, a family doctor meant just that, a physician who was a part of your family. Someone who was a witness to your body, in its health and suffering, over time.

This is how my uncle knew, when our neighbour Mrs. Girardi had chest pain after the death of her daughter, that she wasn't suffering from heart disease but from something much more elemental: grief.

He didn't have an echocardiogram or an ECG in his office to verify this; he listened to her heart with a stethoscope. But more important, he'd been listening to her recount her life for years. There was a kind of communion of trust and healing that took place between doctors and patients. Medicine was a science *and* an art, where hand-holding, even love, were part of the mix.

In his book *The Lost Art of Healing*, Dr. Bernard Lown discusses how he attempts to discover a silver lining when dealing with patients, even in the cloudiest of situations. "This has little to do with truth or falsehood," he wrote. "It flows from the deepest intention of doctoring, to help a patient cope when a condition is hopeless and to recover whenever it is remotely possible."[1]

Remembering the clinical optimism of his role model, Dr. Samuel A. Levine, Lown tells how Levine always finished a consultation by placing his hand on his patient's shoulder and quietly confiding, "You'll be all right."

Levine told Lown, "When a physician offers a grave prognosis or, worse still, when he indicates that the patient is going to die—and miscalculates—the entire medical profession suffers greatly. It is generally best to leave the door a little ajar, even under the darkest circumstances."

Beyond the power of our most sophisticated medical equipment is a physician's humanity—the listening ear, the healing touch, the devices of healers throughout time.

We are all sorely aware of how this tradition has been altered and at what cost. It is difficult to experience a memorable healing encounter when X-rays, catheterizations, and endoscopies are often the main "sites" of interaction between patients and physicians.

Many modern physicians have developed a mechanic's mentality, viewing their function as swiftly finding then fixing a problem rather than fostering a long-term relationship. The pressure of today's health care system to maximize productivity by seeing more patients in less time often causes physicians to focus their attention on technical areas, depriving patients of the chance to tell their stories. Since the real reason for a patient's visit may not be revealed until he has brought up two or three ancillary items, this is a crucial issue.[2]

As Dr. Jerry Vannatta, former dean of the University of Oklahoma College of Medicine, says, "Technology has become a religion within the medical community. It is easy to lose sight of the fact that still, in the 21st century, it is believed that 80 to 85 percent of the diagnosis is in the patient's story."[3]

It's hard to underestimate how much a physician's manner and demeanour have the power to heal or harm. During my training, I remember a middle-aged businessman who was rushed into the catheterization lab in the midst of a heart attack. His wife was talking anxiously in the hallway to the attending cardiologist, whose first contact with the patient was going to be chiefly mechanical—inserting a catheter into his groin for an angioplasty to unblock a major artery. While I stood in the lab trying to calm the patient, the physician burst in, red-faced, ECG results in hand. "Your wife just told me that you smoke and that you just had fried chicken for dinner! What kind of an idiot are you? If you're not taking care of yourself, you deserve to have a heart attack!"

The patient, already ashen, visibly blanched at the physician's tone, one so harsh that I registered it in my own body; I couldn't imagine a more damaging encounter for this patient.

The next morning on rounds, the patient looked paler than ever.

"Is Dr. James with you?" he asked when I entered his room.

"No, just me this morning."

He sighed. "Good, I felt like putting garlic outside the door to keep him away. I never want to see him again."

These two men, strangers to each other, were linked only for an hour, yet their interaction left a long-lasting, deeply negative impression. Indeed, I later found out that the patient failed to keep his follow-up appointment with the attending physician. The chance to build any kind of therapeutic relationship had been lost.

In the long term, I've learned that patients are motivated not by fear but by caring.

Mrs. Ito, a Japanese woman in her sixties, came to see me after a bout of weakness and dizziness that had sent her to the local emergency room. The admitting clerk had difficulty understanding Mrs. Ito's broken English, but when she clutched at her heart, as if she might be having a heart attack, she was rushed into a cubicle.

A young physician followed her in and brusquely examined her, then performed an ECG and a battery of blood tests.

Later, the physician returned to her with her test results and announced abruptly: "Your blood pressure is off the chart! It's very high, very dangerous. You're going to have a stroke unless you control it. A stroke, you understand what that is? You can die."

Mrs. Ito understood perfectly well. In fact, this dire pronouncement was the prime piece of information she held on to when she left the emergency room.

A widow who supported herself by a low-paying job without health insurance, Mrs. Ito was devastated by this diagnosis and convinced that she didn't have adequate resources for her own care. In the weeks that followed, she quit her job and relied entirely on her enclave of Japanese immigrants for advice and ritualistic healing. She lost weight and began spending much of her day in bed. When her symptoms worsened, a friend convinced her to make an appointment with me.

At our first visit, I was alarmed by her frail look as my nurse assisted her into the office. With her drawn face and shuffling gait, she looked like a walking ghost.

I got out my plastic model of the heart and tried to convey to her in the simplest English what high blood pressure meant. "High blood pressure happens when your blood moves through your arteries at a higher pressure than normal. We're concerned because it can cause damage to your blood vessels and elevate your risk of stroke, kidney failure, and heart disease."

I could tell that this wasn't helping. Her face remained sad and drawn.

She had a Walkman around her neck, and I asked her if I could see it. I popped off the back and pointed to the batteries.

"The flow of blood through your body is like the flow of current through an electrical circuit. Think of your heart as the battery that sends blood throughout your system."

Somehow, this visual model seemed to make more sense to her.

She nodded tentatively and said, "Doctor in ER, he said stroke, he said I die."

"That's a possibility only if you ignore your condition. We're going to deal with it. I'm going to prescribe some relaxation methods for you as well as medication."

She wrung her hands. "But no money! I have no money."

"Let me see what I can do." While she sat there, I made a few phone calls to our resource manager. It turned out that Mrs. Ito was eligible to be seen at a free clinic in her neighbourhood that would provide her with regular exams and free prescription medication.

All in all, it took me two hours to begin to undo the damage of her encounter with the emergency room physician.

The language a physician uses can have a powerful impact not only on patients but also on their loved ones.

A daughter stood with her ill father when he was visited by a physician, who took one glance at the man's swollen face and limbs and said, "Congestive heart failure." Given the fatal sound of this diagnosis, the daughter's instant response was one of anguished certainty that her father was terminal. This was reinforced at the hospital, where the acronym for this condition—CHF—was bandied about by the physicians who hovered around her father's bed.[4]

In fact, heart failure is a common condition that, while chronic, is often treatable, even reversible. It is not even a single disease but a confluence of symptoms and syndromes, including fluid retention and possibly a weakened heart muscle. While serious, it is not the death sentence that the daughter believed it to be.

There are plenty of horror stories of "medical alienation," of doctors who don't remember names, test results delayed or botched, long waits and brusque visits. There are also many stories of miraculous treatments and lives saved by modern technology.

The good news is that in reaction to the remoteness of contemporary medicine, there has been a resurgence of interest in the humanistic skills of old-fashioned doctoring.

Companies such as Comsort in Baltimore train physicians in listening and other communication skills. Medical journals such as *Literature and Medicine* and *Journal of Narrative and Life History* focus on the importance of psychosocial factors in health.[5]

To help doctors become more attentive and compassionate, Columbia University and other colleges across the country have instituted programs in what has come to be called narrative medicine. These programs teach courses in literature, literary theory, and creative writing to medical students. The term *narrative medicine* was coined by Dr. Rita Charon, an internist who is director of the program at Columbia, who defines it as "medicine practiced with the narrative competence to recognize, absorb, interpret and be moved by the stories of illness."[6]

One of the reflective writing exercises Charon encourages as part of professional training is called the parallel chart, a kind of personal diary in which a medical student or doctor discusses her feelings about a particular patient and eventually shares these emotions with her peers.

Charon says: "Students and doctors write about their own anguish in caring for patients as well as their victory when things go well, their rage and mourning and dread, their fear of mistakes, their inability to know what to do, their sense of loss as patients sicken, no matter what they do. And when students or doctors read to one another what they have written in the Parallel Chart, they take heart that they are not alone in their sadness and their dread."[7]

"Everyone wants a doctor who's a mensch," says Dr. Jerome Groopman. "Medical schools are searching for structures to produce more empathic physicians." Groopman himself served as an adviser at Harvard Medical School in a program that requires each student to pen a book about a patient and his or her disease.[8]

Experts are also looking again at something as seemingly intuitive as a physician's "bedside manner"—a way of being with a person while imparting trust, sympathy, and authority all at the same time. Research suggests that this is a commodity sorely missed: In one study, nearly 50 percent of a thousand breast cancer patients stated that their physician's explanation of their condition, diagnosis, and treatment had been hard to understand, incomplete, or insufficient. Nearly 60 percent of these same patients wished to have more communication with the medical staff.[9]

There are welcome attempts to reinvent medicine as a listening art—to bring back the skills my uncle used so intuitively, so that patients won't flee the offices of traditional physicians with a fistful of prescriptions and head straight to non–medical professionals in order to find receptive listeners.

This is not to suggest that my uncle—and other old-school physicians—would not be thrilled by the technological marvels we now have at our fingertips. My uncle would have been the first to avail himself of the advanced computerized tomography (CT) heart scan, for example—a noninvasive imaging tool that can take a virtual tour of the heart. The scan peers into the heart and arteries in real time, then displays their condition on an on-screen monitor. In less than thirty minutes, it is possible to detect blockage and ascertain blood flow and heart muscle strength. This can all be accomplished with a simple IV, without the discomfort or risk of more invasive procedures.

Just as crucial, these scans are able to detect the earliest signs of coronary disease years before patients are symptomatic by measuring calcium deposits in the vessel wall. This calcium score can be performed in approximately ten seconds, without an IV, making it as easy as having an X-ray.[10]

My uncle would have been even more excited about the ability to predict disease years before patients develop symptoms by viewing them in the most intimate way possible—on the genetic level.

We each possess a million genetic polymorphisms or single changes in our DNA, which make us, like snowflakes, unique and genetically discrete. Now that researchers have completed the first survey of the entire human genome, it is clear that there are a number of chromosomal regions that contain genetic keys to susceptibility to a variety of illnesses.[11]

For example, the Pima Indians in the southwest United States have a high rate of obesity and type 2 diabetes that has been linked to the "thrifty gene." This gene, favoured in Native Americans through natural selection, protected them against starvation, allowing their bodies to store fat efficiently and survive during times of scarcity and famine. But once their lifestyle was altered and they were placed in a culture of fast food and high fat, the results were disastrous.

We can now gaze directly into biochemical pathways, with an understanding of what is occurring in our cells. In the not so distant future, it is plausible to imagine a scenario in which a technician takes a quick blood sample and within minutes informs a patient about his or her future risk of illness.

We are entering the age of personalized medicine in which our genetic code will guide our choices in diet, medication, and supplement use. The ability to tailor powerful new pharmaceuticals, nutritional programs, and diagnostics to an individual's unique needs will shift the medical paradigm from a disease-care system focused on symptoms and crisis to one focused on prevention and early detection.

My vision of medicine is one that is as strong in compassion as it is in science, that fuses these miraculous new technologies with the ancient healing virtues of the past.

Which brings me to Stu.

At the age of eighty-six, Stu was a longtime, beloved patient, a former jazz musician who was gregarious and relentlessly upbeat, no matter what life dished out to him. During the time I'd known him, he'd lost his wife, his longtime home, and many of his closest friends, but you would never have known it by his cheerful manner.

Whenever I asked, "How're you doing, Stu?" he answered, "Not bad for an old man!"

Given his arterial blockage and weakened heart, we had managed to keep him alive far longer than any of his other doctors had predicted. I saw his survival as a collaboration between the two of us—his love of life and fierce spirit merged with my perseverance and toolbox of procedures and medications. I had deep admiration for him as a brave and caring person who was always willing to lend a helping hand, even when he had difficulty walking.

Stu was a reminder to me of the innate healing powers my patients possessed, powers that needed to be nurtured, encouraged, and evoked whenever possible.

One afternoon Stu came to my office for a surgical clearance; he was scheduled to have a procedure to repair his forearm tendon. At the time of our appointment, his middle finger was dangling, unable to straighten.

"I gotta get this thing fixed. How am I going to throw my fastball?"

"I see your point," I joked, but underneath I was worried. Given his multiple medical problems, I wasn't happy with the idea of his undergoing anesthesia and surgery.

I stalled, looking at his records. "Listen, Stu, how would you feel about me giving you a healing touch treatment?"

"Healing touch? That sounds like some New Age thing."

"Not at all—in fact, it's ancient; it dates back to Hippocrates. It's based on the idea that the body, mind, and emotions form a field of energy. When you're healthy, the energy field is ordered—when there's illness, the energy field is disrupted."

He seemed surprised at my explanation. "And *you* would do this for me yourself?"

I nodded.

He shrugged and smiled. "I'm game. Especially if it doesn't hurt."

For the next twenty minutes, I forgot about the incidentals of his medical history—his HDL level and his vexing blockages—and focussed instead on his great reservoir of strength as well as my own love for him and hope that this surgery would go well. For a bit of time that August morning, I perceived us as two fields of light and energy, joined together.

A week later, I was relieved when my secretary told me that Stu was on the phone.

"How was the surgery?"

"Well, that's what I'm calling to tell you. I didn't need it. The day after you did your treatment, my hand returned to normal. The surgery was cancelled. I feel great."

My rational medical mind immediately began scurrying around for reasons for this healing. Surely it was the result of decreased inflammation, an internal healing of scar tissue, anything but what was being implied. And then I stopped myself. It dawned on me that I didn't need to do this anymore.

The split that existed between modern technology and ancient healing had finally fused in me. My career has been the fruit of that union.

References

Chapter 1: The Unexamined Heart

1. Stewart Wolf and John G. Bruhn, *Roseto Story: An Anatomy of Health* (Norman: University of Oklahoma Press, 1979).

2. Stewart Wolf and John G. Bruhn, *The Power of Clan: The Influence of Human Relationships on Heart Disease* (Somerset, NJ: TransactionPublishers, 1992).

3. Edward O. Wilson, *Biophilia* (Cambridge, MA: Harvard University Press, 1986).

4. G. A. Kaplan, "Alameda County [California] Health and Ways of Living Study," 1974 PANEL [Computer file], ICPSR version (Berkeley, CA: Human Population Laboratory, California Department of Health Services [producer], 1974. Ann Arbor, MI: Interuniversity Consortium for Political and Social Research [distributor], 1996).

5. G. A. Kaplan et al., "Social Connection and Mortality from All Causes and from Cardiovascular Disease: Prospective Evidence from Eastern Finland," *American Journal of Epidemiology* 128 (1988): 370–80.

6. W. Ruberman, E. Weinblatt, J. D. Goldberg, and B. S. Chaudhary, "Psychosocial Influences on Mortality After Myocardial Infarction," *New England Journal of Medicine* 31 (August 30, 1984): 552–59. A. Kagan, G. G. Rhoads, P. D. Zeegen, and M. Z. Nichaman, "Coronary Heart Disease Among Men of Japanese Ancestry in Hawaii. The Honolulu Heart Study," Israeli Journal of Medical Science 7 (1971): 1573–77.

7. Gregg Easterbrook, *The Progress Paradox* (New York: Random House, 2003).
8. Heart Health, Franklin Institute, www.sln.fi.edu/biosci/heart.html.

Chapter 3: The Fog of Stress

1. Heart Disease and Stroke Statistics Update, American Heart Association, 2003.
2. M. de Lorgeril, M. P. Salen, J. L. Martin, I. Monjaud, J. Delaye, and N. Mamelle, "Mediterranean Diet, Traditional Risk Factors, and the Rate of Cardiovascular Complications After Myocardial Infarction: Final Report of the Lyon Diet Heart Study," *Circulation* 99 (1999): 779–85.
3. Kimberly Williams, "Mindfulness Training Program and Yoga," *American Journal of Health Promotion*, July 2001.
4. H. Eysenck, "Psychosocial Factors, Cancer and Ischaemic Heart Disease," *British Journal of Medical Psychology* 61 (1988).
5. American Institute of Stress, www.stress.org/problem.
6. T. G. Allison, D. E. Williams, et al., "Medical and Economic Costs of Psychologic Distress in Patients with Coronary Heart Disease," *Mayo Clinic Proceedings* 70 (1995): 8.
7. L. J. van Doomen and K. F. Orlebeke, "Stress, Personality and Serum-Cholesterol Level," *Journal of Human Stress* 8 (December 1982): 24–29.
8. T. Theorell and B. Floderus-Myrhed, " 'Workload' and Risk of Myocardial Infarction: A Prospective Psychosocial Analysis," *International Journal of Epidemiology* 6, no. 1 (1977): 17–21.
9. Paul Teirstein et al., "Catheter-based Radiotherapy to Inhibit Restenosis After Coronary Stenting," *New England Journal of Medicine* 336 (1997): 1697–1703.
10. Herbert Benson, Julie Croliss, and Geoffrey Cowley, "Brain Check," *Newsweek*, September 27, 2004.
11. Dean Ornish, *Reversing Heart Disease* (New York: Ballantine Books, 1990).

12. Rainer Maria Rilke, "Archaic Torso of Apollo," in *The Selected Poetry of Rainer Maria Rilke*, trans. Stephen Mitchell (New York: Vintage, 1989).

13. Thornton Wilder, *Our Town* (New York: Samuel French Inc., 1997); originally produced in 1938.

Chapter 4: Echoes of Anger

1. Raymond Niaura et al., "Hostility, the Metabolic Syndrome, and Incident Coronary Heart Disease," *Health Psychology* 21, no. 6 (2002).

2. M. Friedman and R. H. Rosenman, "Association of Overt Behavior Pattern with Blood and Cardiovascular Findings," *Journal of the American Medical Association* 169 (1959): 1286–96.

3. Edward C. Suarez, "Joint Effect of Hostility and Severity of Depressive Symptoms on Plasma Interleukin-6 Concentration," *Psychosomatic Medicine* 65 (2003): 523–27.

4. C. Iribarren et al., "Association of Hostility with Coronary Artery Calicification in Young Adults: The CARDIA Study," *Journal of the American Medical Association* 283 (May 17, 2000):2546–51.

5. Elaine D. Eaker et al., "Anger and Hostility Predict the Development of Atrial Fibrillation in Men in the Framingham Offspring Study," *Circulation* 109 (2004): 1267–71.

6. Howard B. Beckman and Richard M. Frankel, "The Effect of Physician Behavior on the Collection of Data," *Annals of Internal Medicine* 101 (1984): 692–96.

7. David Mechanic et al., "Are Patients' Office Visits with Physicians Getting Shorter?," *New England Journal of Medicine* 344 (January 18, 2001): 198–204 .

8. Chuck Appleby, "Getting Doctors to Listen to Patients," *Managed Care* 12 (1996).

9. James Pennebaker and J. Seagal, "Forming a Story: The Health Benefits of Narrative," *Journal of Clinical Psychology* 55, no. 10 (1999): 1243–54.

10. David Maybury-Lewis, *Millennium*, video series, Telefilms

Canada.

11. Pennebaker and Seagal, "Forming a Story."

12. Dean Ornish, *Reversing Heart Disease* (New York: Ballantine Books, 1990).

Chapter 5: The Landscape of Depression

1. Galen, *On the Usefulness of the Parts of the Body*, trans. Margaret Tallmadge May (Ithaca, NY: Cornell University Press, 1968).

2. Leonardo da Vinci, "A History of the Heart," www.stanford.edu/class/history.

3. World Health Organization, "The World Health Report 2001: Mental Health: New Understanding, New Hope" (Geneva: World Health Organization, 2001).

4. James J. Lynch, *A Cry Unheard: New Insights into the Medical Consequences of Loneliness* (Baltimore: Bancroft Press, 2000).

5. Gregg Easterbrook, *The Progress Paradox* (New York: Random House, 2003).

6. Lynch, *A Cry Unheard*.

7. A. Appels, "Depression and Coronary Heart Disease: Observations and Questions," *Journal of Psychosomatic Research* 43 (November 1997): 443–52; review.

8. N. Frasure-Smith, F. Lesperance, and M. Talajic, "Depression and 18-Month Prognosis After Myocardial Infarction," *Circulation* 91 (April 1995): 999–1005.

9. M. D. Sullivan, A. Z. LaCroix, C. Baum, L. C. Grothaus, and W. Katon, "Functional Status in Coronary Artery Disease: A One-Year Prospective Study of the Role of Anxiety and Depression," *American Journal of Medicine* 103 (November 1997): 348–56.

10. L. G. Russek and G. E. Schwartz, "Interpersonal Heart-Brain Registration and the Perception of Parental Love: A 42-year Follow-up of the Harvard Mastery of Stress Study," *Subtle Energies* 5 (1994): 195.

11. F. Lesperance, N. Frasure-Smith, and M. Talajic, "Major Depression Before and After Myocardial Infarction: Its

Nature and Consequences," *Psychosomatic Medicine* 58 (1996): 99–110.

12. D. C. Steffens, M. J. Helms, K. Krishnan, and G. L. Burke, "Cere-brovascular Disease and Depression Symptoms in the Cardiovascular Health Study," *Stroke* 30 (1999): 2159–66.

13. Alexander H. Glassman et al., "Sertraline Treatment of Major Depression in Patients with Acute MI or Unstable Angina," *Journal of the American Medical Association* 288 (2002): 701–9.

14. Ibid.

15. "Golden Year Blues," *DukeMed News*, Fall 2002, www.dukehealth.org.

16. James J. Lynch, *The Language of the Heart: The Human Body in Dialogue* (New York: Basic Books, 1985).

17. Gregg Easterbrook, *The Progress Paradox* (New York: Random House, 2004).

18. Martin Seligman, *Learned Optimism: How to Change Your Mind and Your Life* (New York: Free Press, 1998).

19. Glassman et al., "Sertraline Treatment of Major Depression in Patients with Acute MI or Unstable Angina."

20. Oakley Ray, "How the Mind Hurts and Heals the Body," *American Psychologist* 59, no. 1 (2004).

21. L. D. Kubzansky, D. Sparrow, P. Vokonas, and I. Kawachi, "Is the Glass Half Empty or Half Full? A Prospective Study of Optimism and Coronary Heart Disease in the Normative Aging Study," *Psychosomatic Medicine* 63 (2001): 910–16.

22. K. A. Matthews, K. Raikkonen, K. Sutton-Tyrrell, and L. H. Kuller, "Optimistic Attitudes Protect Against Progression of Carotid Atherosclerosis in Healthy Middle-aged Women," *Psychosomatic Medicine* 66 (September/October 2004): 640–44.

23. Seligman, *Learned Optimism*.

24. Robert Emmons and Michael McCullough, eds., *The Psychology of Gratitude* (New York: Oxford University Press, 2004).

25. Everett L. Worthington, "Empirical Research in Forgive-

ness: Looking Backward, Looking Forward." In Everett L. Worthington, ed., *Dimensions of Forgiveness: Psychological Research and Theological Perspectives* (Philadelphia: Templeton Foundation Press, 1998), 321–39.

26. R. D. Enright, E. A. Gassin, and C. Wu, "Forgiveness: A Developmental View," *Journal of Moral Education* 21 (1992): 99–114.

27. Jordana Lewis and Jerry Adler, "Forgive and Let Live," *Newsweek*, September 27, 2004.

28. C. V. O. Witvliet, T. E. Ludwig, and K. L. Vander Laan, "Granting Forgiveness or Harboring Grudges: Implications for Emotion, Physiology, and Health," *Psychological Science* 121 (2001): 117–23.

29. Lewis and Adler, "Forgive and Let Live."

30. Marianne Williamson, *A Return to Love* (New York: HarperCollins, 1996).

31. Peter Rabins, Getting Old Without *Getting Anxious* (New York: Putnam, 2004.).

Chapter 6: Sacred Revelations

1. Jeffery L. Sheler, "The Power of Prayer," *U.S. News & World Report*, December 20, 2004.

2. Donna Gehrke-White, "Link Between Faith, Health Gets More Attention," Knight Ridder Newspapers, June 12, 2004.

3. Nancy Waring, "Can Prayer Heal?" *Hippocrates* 14, no. 8, www.hippocrates.com/archive/August 2000.

4. Larry Dossey, *Healing Words: The Power of Prayer and the Practice of Medicine* (San Francisco: HarperCollins, 1993).

5. F. Sicher et al., "A Randomized Double Blind Study of the Effect of Distant Healing in a Population with Advanced AIDS: Report of a Small Scale Study," *Western Journal of Medicine* 169 (1998): 356–63.

6. R. C. Byrd, "Positive Therapeutic Effects of Intercessory Prayer in a Coronary Care Unit Population," *Southern Medical Journal* 81 (1988): 826–29.

7. Mitchell Krucoff, "MANTRA" (Monitor and Actu-

alization of Noetic Trainings), for presentation at the seventy-first annual scientific sessions of the American Heart Association (AHA), 1998.

8. Franklin Loehr, *The Power of Prayer on Plants* (New York: New American Library, 1959).

9. Jeffery L. Sheler, "The Power of Prayer," *U.S. News & World Report*.

10. Ibid.

11. A. Newberg and J. Iversen, "The Neural Basis of the Complex Mental Task of Meditation: Neurotransmitter and Neurochemical Considerations," *Medical Hypotheses* 61 (2003): 282–91.

12. A. Gregory, "When Science and Christianity Meet," *Journal of the American Medical Association* 291 (2004): 2875–76.

13. Andrew Weil, "Can Spirituality Affect Healing?," www.drweil.com.

14. Herbert Benson and Miriam Z. Klipper, *The Relaxation Response*, reissue edition (New York: HarperTorch, 1976).

15. Annie Murphy, "Reality Goes Under the Knife," *Psychology Today*, March/April 1998.

16. Dossey, *Healing Words*.

Chapter 7: The Persistence of Grief

1. "Death from a Broken Heart," WebMD, November 24, 2003, http://my.webmd.com/content/article/77/95 423 .htm.

2. Taylor Fogarty, "Country Music Artists Pay Tribute to Johnny Cash," *American Western*, September 2003.

3. M. Mittelman, "American Heart Association Conference on Cardiovascular Disease and Epidemiology," *Family Practice News* 26 (April 15, 1996): 8.

4. R. H. Rosenman, "Does Anxiety or Cardiovascular Reactivity Have a Causal Role," *Integrative Physiological and Behavioral Science* 26 (1991): 296–304.

5. T. R. Dawber, The Framingham Study: *The Epidemiology of Atherosclerotic Disease* (Cambridge, MA: Harvard Uni-

versity Press, 1980).

6. The Centre for Genetics Education, www.genetics.com.au.

7. *Dialogues of the Buddha*, trans. T. W. Rhys Davids (London: Oxford University Press, 1899).

8. J. Li, D. H. Precht, P. B. Mortenson, and J. Olsen, "Mortality in Parents After Death of a Child in Denmark: A Nationwide Followup Study," *Lancet* 361 (February 1, 2003): 363–67.

9. Ilan Wittstein, "Neurohumoral Features of Myocardial Stunning Due to Sudden Emotional Stress," *New England Journal of Medicine* 352 (February 10, 2005): 539–48.

10. Elisabeth Kübler-Ross. *On Death and Dying*, reprint edition (New York: Scribner's, 1997).

11. Swami Vivekananda, *Complete Works of Swami Vivekananda*, 8th ed. (Calcutta: Advaita Ashrama, 1999).

12. Gregg Easterbrook, *The Progress Paradox* (New York: Random House, 2003).

13. Wayne Muller, "Questions That Matter," *Noetic Sciences Review*, Spring 1998.

Chapter 8: The Little Brain

1. J. I. and B. C. Lacey, "Two-way Communication Between the Heart and the Brain: Significance of Time Within the Cardiac Cycle," *American Psychologist* (February 1978): 99–103.

2. J. A. Armour and J. Ardell, eds., *Neurocardiology* (New York: Oxford University Press, 1994).

3. Raymond Faulkner, trans., *The Egyptian Book of the Dead: The Book of Going Forth by Day* (New York: Chronicle Books, 2000).

4. Hazrat Inayat Khan, *The Art of Being and Becoming* (New York: Omega Publications, 1989).

5. R. K. French, "The Thorax in History: From Ancient Times to Aristotle," *Thorax* 33 (1978): 10–18.

6. Plato, *Timaeus*, trans. F. M. Cornford (New York: Mac-

millan, 1959).

7. Research Overview, HeartMath Research Center, Boulder Creek, CA.

8. Walter Cannon, "Voodoo Death," *American Anthropologist* 44 (1942): 169–81.

9. I. Kawachi, D. Sparrow, A. Spiro, P. S. Vokonas, and S. T. Weiss, "A Prospective Study of Anger and Coronary Heart Disease," *Circulation* 94 (1996): 2092–95.

10. R. Grossarth-Maticek, H. J. Eysenck, et al., "Personality Type, Smoking Habit and Their Interaction as Predictors of Cancer and Coronary Heart Disease," *Personality and Individual Differences* 9 (1988): 479–95.

11. M. Mittelman, American Heart Association Sixty-seventh Scientific Sessions, 1994.

12. "The Heart, a Mind of Its Own," Universal Tao, www.universaltao.com.

13. Larry Dossey, *Healing Words: The Power of Prayer and the Practice of Medicine* (San Francisco: HarperCollins, 1993).

14. Jeff Levin, *God, Faith, and Health: Exploring the Spirituality–Healing Connection* (New York: John Wiley, 2001).

15. Glen Reid et al., "The Physiological and Psychological Effects of Compassion and Anger," *Journal of Advancement in Medicine* 8 (1995): 87–105.

16. Research Overview, HeartMath Research Center, Boulder Creek, CA.

17. "Health for Life," *Newsweek*, September 27, 2004.

18. Ibid.

19. Aaron Antonovsky, *Unraveling the Mystery of Health: How People Manage Stress and Stay Well* (New York: Jossey-Bass, 1987).

20. Rob Stein, "Study: Women's Heart Health Neglected," *Washington Post*, February 2, 2005.

21. National Heart Association Survey, 2000.

22. Stein, "Study: Women's Heart Health Neglected."

23. Jean McSweeney et al., "Women's Early Warning Symptoms of Acute Myocardial Infarction," *Circulation* 108 (2003): 2619.

24. Ibid.

25. Ibid.

26. Mauro Moscucci et al., American Heart Association Scientific Sessions, Abstract Oral Presentation, Session 98.1, Abstract 2692. Blue Cross Blue Shield of Michigan Cardiovascular Consortium, November 9, 2004.

27. Women's Heart Foundation, www.womensheartfoundation.org.

Chapter 9: Universal Heart

1. Alan Watts, *Myself: A Case of Mistaken Identity* (San Anselmo, CA: Audio Wisdom, 1973).

2. Larry Dossey, *Reinventing Medicine: Beyond Mind-Body to a New Era of Healing* (San Francisco: HarperCollins, 1999).

3. Larry Dossey, *Healing Words: The Power of Prayer and the Practice of Medicine* (San Francisco: HarperCollins, 1993).

4. F. Sicher et al., "A Randomized Double Blind Study of the Effect of Distant Healing in a Population with Advanced AIDS: Report of a Small Scale Study," *Western Journal of Medicine* 169 (1998): 356–63.

5. Paul Pearsall, *The Heart's Code* (New York: Broadway Books, 1998).

6. P. Pearsall, G. E. Schwartz, and L. G. Russek, "Changes in Heart Transplant Recipients That Parallel the Personalities of Their Donors," *Integrative Medicine* 2 (2000): 65–72.

7. Personal communication to Paul Pearsall.

Chapter 10: Toward Compassionate Medicine

1. Bernard Lown, *The Lost Art of Healing* (New York: Ballantine Books, 1996).

2. Chuck Appleby, "Getting Doctors to Listen to Patients," *Managed Care Magazine* 12 (1996).

3. Dinitia Smith, "Diagnosis Goes Low Tech," *New York Times*, October 16, 2003.

4. Susanna E. Bedell, Thomas B. Graboys, Elizabeth Bedell, and Bernard Lown, "Words That Harm, Words That Heal," *Archives of Internal Medicine* 164 (July 12, 2004).

5. Appleby, "Getting Doctors to Listen to Patients."

6. Melanie Thernstrom, "The Writing Cure," *New York Times*, April 18, 2004.

7. Rita Charon, LitSite Alaska, http://litsite.alaska.edu/uaa/healing/medicine.html.

8. Thernstrom, "The Writing Cure."

9. William Campbell Douglass II, "Listen to the Patient, Real Health Daily Dose," April 4, 2003, www.realhealth-news.com.

10. News about Inner Imaging, www.innerimaging.com.

11. Zubenko et al., "Genome-wide Linkage Survey for Genetic Loci That Influence the Development of Depressive Disorders in Families with Recurrent, Early-Onset Major Depression," *American Journal of Medical Genetics*, Part B: *Neuropsychiatric Genetics* 123B (November 2003): 1–18.

Further Reading

Borysenko, J. *Minding the Body, Mending the Mind*. New York: Bantam Books, 1988.

Brennan, Barbara. *Hands of Light: A Guide to Healing Through the Human Energy Field*. New York: Bantam, 1988.

Chopra, Deepak. *Quantum Healing*. New York: Bantam Books, 1989.

De Salvo, Louise. *Writing as a Way of Healing: How Telling Our Stories Transforms Our Lives*. San Francisco: HarperCollins, 1999.

Dossey, Larry. *Healing Words: The Power of Prayer and the Practice of Medicine*. San Francisco: HarperCollins, 1993.

————. *Reinventing Medicine: Beyond Mind-Body to a New Era of Healing*. San Francisco: HarperCollins, 1999.

Easwaran, Eknath. *Meditation: Commensense Directions for an Uncommon Life*. Berkeley, CA: The Blue Mountain Center of Meditation, 1978.

Emoto, Masaru. *The Hidden Messages in Water*. Hillsboro, OR: Beyond Words Publishing, 2001.

Gawande, Atul. *Complications: A Surgeon's Notes on an Imperfect Science.*
New York: Picador, 2002.

Goldberg, Nieca. *Women Are Not Small Men: Life-saving Strategies for Preventing and Healing Heart Disease in Women.* New York: Ballantine, 2003.

Gordon, Richard, Eleanor Barrow, and Carrie Toder, illustrators. *Quantum Touch: The Power to Heal.* Berkeley: North Atlantic Books, 2002.

Groopman, Jerome. *The Anatomy of Hope.* New York: Random House, 2004.

Kabat-Zinn, Jon. *Full Catastrophe Living: A Practical Guide to Mindfulness, Meditation, and Healing.* New York: Delacorte Press, 1990.

Langer, E. J. *Mindfulness.* New York: Addison-Wesley, 1989.

Laskow, Leonard. *Healing with Love.* New York: HarperCollins, 1992.

Lown, Bernard. *The Lost Art of Healing.* New York: Ballantine, 1996.

Lynch, James. *A Cry Unheard: New Insights into the Medical Consequences of Loneliness.* Baltimore: Bancroft Press, 2000.

———. *The Language of the Heart: The Body's Response to Human Dialogue.* New York: Basic Books, 1985.

Muller, Wayne. *How Then, Shall We Live?: Four Simple Questions That Reveal the Beauty and Meaning of Our Lives.* New York: Bantam, 1997.

————. *Learning How to Pray: How We Find Heaven on Earth*. New York: Bantam, 2003.

Nelson, Miriam E., and Alice Lichtenstein. *Strong Women, Strong Hearts*. New York: Putnam, 2005.

Newberg, Andrew, Eugene G. D'Aquili, and Vince Rause. *Why God Won't Go Away*. London: Ballantine Books, 2001.

Nuland, Sherwin. *How We Die: Reflections on Life's Final Chapter*. New York: Vintage, 1995.

Ofri, Danielle. *Singular Intimacies: Becoming a Doctor at Bellevue*. Boston: Beacon Press, 2003.

Ornish, Dean. *Love and Survival: The Basis for the Healing Power of Intimacy*. New York: HarperCollins, 1998.

————. *Reversing Heart Disease*. New York: Ballantine, 1990.

Oyle, I. *The Healing Mind*. Berkeley, CA: Celestial Arts, 1974.

Oz, Mehmet, and Lisa Oz. *Healing from the Heart: A Leading Surgeon Combines Eastern and Western Traditions to Create the Medicine of the Future*. New York: Plume, 1999.

Pearsall, Paul. *The Heart's Code*. New York: Broadway Books, 1998.

Pert, Candace. *Molecules of Emotion: The Science Behind Mind-Body Medicine*. New York: Scribner's, 1999.

Rossman, M. L. *Healing Yourself*. New York: Pocket Books, 1987.

Sacks, Oliver. *Awakenings*. New York: Vintage, 1999.